PRAISE FOR LAUNCH THEM WELL

Launching our children well is a journey that has to begin long before they actually fly on their own. The letting go process requires us to separate our identities as moms from our children's lives and entrust them to the Creator who gave them to us in the first place. If you know you need to do that but aren't sure how, Cristina offers the perspective and practical next steps you need.

Jill Savage
Relationship Coach, Speaker, and Author of *Empty Nest Full Life*

This profound book is filled with inspiring stories, wise insights, and practical tools to prepare you to launch your children well. It's the book I wish had been available many years ago when both our daughters headed off to college. I love how each chapter ends with "How's Your Heart" questions that will encourage you to go through this book with a community of other moms on the same journey.

Judy Dunagan
Author of *The Loudest Roar: Living in the Unshakable Victory of Christ*

Our goal as parents is to raise independent, healthy adults; but oftentimes, we get bogged down in the details of our current parenting season and forget to look ahead at how to reach our goal. Cristina offers practical, tangible ways to make sure the day the clock strikes eighteen doesn't sneak up on us. This book is a great guide to help you think through not only how to prepare your children for adulting but also the important work of preparing your heart to launch them well.

Jill Comer
Mom of four (75% launched)

From the moment our children are born, we are on a journey to raise them to be confident and independent adults. But how do we get there? Cristina offers practical ideas and strategies for raising and releasing them while building a relationship of mutual respect and grace for mistakes as we move into the parenting phase of empowering healthy adult children.

Jen Jacobsen
Empty nest mom of two

LAUNCH THEM WELL

A JOURNEY OF LETTING GO FOR MOMS

CRISTINA WRIGHT

Publisher Information:
An Apt Word, Ltd.
Colorado Springs, CO

For more information or to contact the author, please email anaptword@gmail.com.

ISBN 979-8-9917261-0-8 (eBook)
ISBN 979-8-9917261-1-5 (softcover)
ISBN 979-8-9917261-2-2 (hardcover)

Cover design: Terry Dugan
Cover photo credit: Cagkan@Adobe Stock
Editorial Team: Marcus Costantino and Amy Sinnott
Interior design: Ben Wolf, Inc.
Publishing services provided by BelieversBookServices.com

First printing: 2024

Printed in the United States of America

To Mom and Dad, for being the banks to my river.

And to Mrs. Peggy Hailes, for being the first to believe in my dream.

CONTENTS

INTRODUCTION

Near my Colorado hometown, there's a hike called the Manitou Incline. It is rated "extreme," and they aren't kidding! The hike is just under a mile with 2,744 steps, an elevation gain of 2,020 feet (in under a mile!), and a grade that ranges from 41% - 68%. (And I think it's worth noting: After reaching the summit, most hikers take Barr Trail down, which is a fairly steep 3.6-mile hike through switchbacks to the base of the mountain.) Did I mention it was extreme?

I had done the hike twice in my 40s, and a decade had passed since my last summit when my fifteen-year-old son asked me to hike it with him. Of course, I said yes! I'll cut to the chase: It was hard! And I knew it would be hard from previous experience, but this time it felt punishing. I was slow —much slower than the last time I had hiked it. But I wasn't in it for speed; I was in it to finish.

The thing I love about hiking the Incline is the community. It is a hard hike for every single person on the mountain, regardless of speed. Some do it in thirty minutes (like my son), and others take a couple of hours or more to summit. But everyone encourages each other. And everyone is out there for different reasons. Some are hiking for fitness; others are hiking to challenge themselves. I met a seventy-six-year-old man hiking it for the first time with his granddaughters. And I met a couple in their 40s who were hiking to honor their son who had died the previous year. On the Incline, you meet people and quickly become kindred spirits for those difficult steps you are taking to get to the top.

I had to stop often to catch my breath, and I began to think about the encouragement I received from others and the encouragement I gave. At one point, with each step, my mantra became, "I can do hard things." During one of my breaks, I shared that with a young girl who replied, "We *get* to do this!" I loved her perspective!

And just like hiking the Incline—for the first time or tenth time—launching our children into adulthood is hard! We can do it alone, but it's much easier if we have a community spurring us on. And no matter how prepared we think we are it will be harder than expected.

At the time of this writing, my husband Tim and I have a twenty-one-year-old daughter who is getting married in nine months and a son who will be sixteen in a few weeks. Our girl is essentially launched, as she is financially independent and succeeding at adulting in a way that is not at all surprising to me and her dad. What is surprising is the angst I feel as we start over in this season of launching with our son. You'd think I've never done this before for all the emotional fumbling I seem to be doing. I want you to know this: I have launched and I am launching—we are on this journey together!

In the pages that follow, you will hear stories of success and failure, love and fear, hope and discouragement. Each chapter ends with a section titled "How's Your Heart," which contains questions meant to evoke introspection about your own journey as a mom, and a section titled, "Embrace Truth" with Bible verses for you to ponder and pray over. We will make it through this season of life one step at a time. We get to do this! Let's do it *well* … together!

1

PERSPECTIVE MATTERS

I have had worse partings, but none that so
Gnaws at my mind still. Perhaps it is roughly
Saying what God alone could perfectly show —
How selfhood begins with a walking away,
And love is proved in the letting go.
C. Day-Lewis

In the final months of her life, my grandma was put in hospice in my parent's home. She was ninety years old, and it was the first time in my life that I was able to spend time with her every week because we had always lived in separate towns. At the same time, my daughter Emma was a senior in high school. I was grieving the inevitable changing of seasons —from a high schooler living at home to a college student living in a different city. There were days I felt like I wouldn't survive her becoming an adult. We had always been close and were becoming friends in her teenage years; I enjoyed spending time with her. I couldn't imagine a day, week, or month when I didn't see her. I knew I was grieving her leaving, but I didn't know how to do it well. Additionally, after a decade of homeschooling my children in varying capacities, my son Nate was preparing to enter full-time high school. Life as I knew it was morphing into something unrecognizable faster than I could comprehend, and I found myself thinking, "I want to launch my children *well*."

As I spent time with my grandma each week, I got to know her as a woman and a mom. It would become the greatest gift I ever received from her. Grandma and I would talk for hours — about her childhood, her marriage, being a mom, serving at church, and the things she enjoyed. I would often tell her about my struggle to let go of my children and I'd say, "Grandma, I don't think I will survive it." She'd hold my hand, look me in the eye, and say, "You're gonna be okay."

After seven months in at-home hospice, my grandma entered her final days. She knew her time was short, and she talked often about seeing Jesus face to face. Every evening before leaving to head home, I would tell her I loved her, and she would tell me she was at peace. But one night I could see she was troubled. I asked her what was wrong, and she said, "I'm not at peace. I know I will be going to heaven soon, and I need to talk to each of my children." I called my dad into the room, her oldest living son, and they talked privately. Then I Facetimed my aunt and uncle, her other two living children, and let her have private conversations with each of them. When she was done, she said she was at peace. She went to heaven three days later.

At ninety years old, with all three of her adult children in their seventies with families of their own, my grandma revealed her mother's heart — to know her children would be okay when she was no longer here. A mom will always be a mom. Our mother hearts never leave us. In witnessing my grandma's last effort to be a mom to her adult children, I felt permission to feel all the emotions of watching my children grow up, to grieve, and to struggle. Of course it would be hard, and it would hurt. But it also would be exciting and fun and a new adventure to watch my children become who God created them to be, to spread their wings and fly, and to become my adult children's friend.

BURDEN OF SURRENDER

I penned the following words in my journal one day when surrender felt especially heavy. It felt like a weight on my chest, blocking the very air I needed to simply survive.

> Why does surrender feel like such a heavy burden? It weighs me down every time I think about it. It feels like a yoke I cannot bear. But Jesus says his yoke is easy and light. Why is this so heavy upon me? But that's the point, isn't it? If I am going to hold onto anyone, I need to hold onto Jesus. Not my kids. In opening my hands in surrender, I am free to grasp onto Jesus' promises. How can I do that if I am tight-fisted and holding onto my children, keeping them from spreading their wings and flying the way I raised them to do? The way I did when I was their age. It's how God intended it. Surrender is not a burden; it's a freedom. Perhaps it only feels heavy because I am trying to do it in my own strength—my own way—instead of giving God room to work and move and speak.

I thought *I shouldn't feel this way.* Then I remembered the words of Jesus in Matthew 11:28-30: "Come to me, all you who are weary and burdened, and I will give you rest. Take my yoke upon you and learn from me, for I am gentle and humble in heart, and you will find rest for your souls. For my yoke is easy and my burden is light." What is Jesus' yoke? He wasn't referring to physical burdens, he was pointing to the law, which the Pharisees were imposing on people to earn salvation. "The 'yoke of the Pharisees' is the burdensome yoke of self-righteousness and legalistic law-keeping. It has been said by biblical scholars that the Pharisees had added over 600 regulations regarding what qualified as 'working' on the Sabbath. That is a heavy burden!"[1] Jesus' yoke is the opposite of the law, that is to say, Jesus' yoke is grace. That's why Paul told the Galatians, "It is for freedom that Christ has set us free. Stand firm, then, and do not let yourselves be burdened again by a yoke of slavery."[2]

So, how does all of this relate to my struggle with letting my children grow up? I wasn't surrendering to God's leading and the grace that awaited me for the difficult season I was in. I was trying so hard to hold onto them and keep things from moving forward (as if I could stop them from growing up) that I was living in my own strength. I wasn't "[looking] to the Lord and his strength."[3] I was only looking inward, not up to the One who could and would carry my burden for me. My rest would be found in surrender. My strength would be found in him.

THE HARDEST PART

I once read, "A mother's job is to teach her children to not need her anymore. The hardest part of that job is accepting success." I have found that to be absolute truth — hard truth.

My daughter was fifteen years old the first time she walked into a college classroom. She attended a dual-enrollment high school and graduated a semester early with two years of college credits. A shockingly short two years later, she graduated college at the age of nineteen with a bachelor's degree. She began a career in finance a year before she graduated and went on to work for that same company as a full-time financial analyst. She also got engaged that same year. My girl — driven, ambitious, and bright. Always on the fast track! It was exciting, and it was jolting!

For me, the hardest part of her success was letting go so she could live as the adult I raised her to become. She was succeeding and maturing and growing into an independent young woman much faster than I anticipated or thought possible. And then there was my son, starting high school in the same dual-enrollment school his sister attended. My boy—fiercely independent, intelligent, and endlessly curious. There was no doubt in my mind that he would reach the same success and independence as his sister, I just secretly hoped he'd do it a little slower. The thing is that I found myself bracing for those empty-nest years long before they were upon me.

We all launch our children into the world, ready or not, one way or another. Some go with angry parting words and the slam of a door. Some go quietly but without guidance or direction. Others go happily with a blessing.

As my daughter progressed through her high school years, and a few years later as my son began his, I found myself thinking often about how to launch them *well*. What does that mean? I wanted them to be empowered to make decisions, equipped to handle difficult people and situations, free to choose their friends, confident to be who God created them to be, and committed to living a life of integrity. That meant I had to let them make decisions. I had to let them fail and learn from their mistakes. I had to let them succeed in their own ways. I had to allow room for the Holy Spirit to talk and lead (ahem … stop talking so he could).

As a homeschool mom for a decade, I studied lots of things with my kids: science, history, math, writing, grammar, and zoology. We did experiments, hiked, took art classes, went on road trips, visited museums, and baked. I'm sure we studied rockets at some point (and that my son could tell you more about them than I ever taught him), but I know very little about rockets and space exploration. The one thing I do know is that it takes significant planning and training—lots of tests and trial and error and equipping—before a rocket is launched. I'm sure this is where the breakdown of my analogy begins, but it occurred to me—we don't just launch our children (and launch them *well*) on the day they leave home for college or a job or whatever that next thing is. Launching our children well begins years before they leave home. Dare I say, it begins incrementally the day they are born? It begins as we teach them how to talk and walk, make little decisions (red or green shirt), how to treat others, clean their rooms, help in the kitchen, and the value of money.

Launching our children well is a process and one that must commence long before they are required to fly on their own. Are we willing to separate our identities as moms from our children's lives and entrust them to the Creator who gave them to us in the first place?

SHIFTING PERSPECTIVE

Imagine looking at a mountain. From the base, it might seem daunting and insurmountable. But from the peak, the view is breathtaking, and the journey to the top is a testament to your strength and perseverance. Perspective transforms the same mountain into two entirely different experiences. And so it is with parenting and the journey of letting go as our children grow into adults.

In my research for this book, I began to see a common theme among the moms I talked with—they were struggling to let go of their children. Even the ones who were intentional about releasing their children into adulthood seemed to struggle. Even the ones who avoided being helicopter moms. Even the ones who trusted God with their children. Even the ones who knew their children were ready to launch. They all struggled with letting go. The one difference was how these moms responded. Some turned to friends for support. Others joined mom groups. And still others leaned into their faith. But some tightened their grip, white-knuckling their children's lives as if they could stop the inevitable from happening. I wonder, was love or fear their motivation? Maybe it was a little—or a lot—of both.

As I was writing about the burden of surrender and pondered the grief I was experiencing as my children grow into young adults, I wondered if there were parents who felt differently. I was certain there would be some who embraced their growing children with nothing but optimism and excitement for them to leave home. Kudos if that's you! But in my experience of talking to parents, from friends to family to strangers, I had not heard that narrative. So, I did what any good writer would do—I Googled it. I typed the words *excited for kids to leave home?* And the first thing that popped up was a pretty well-written poem. I asked Google who wrote it so I could cite it appropriately, and the response was, "I cannot tell you anything about the author of this poem." As I watched the answer being typed out on my screen, I realized I was interacting with Microsoft's new chatbot CoPilot. AI wrote the poem! And the thing is, AI incorporated my question into the poem and led me to the conclusion that even AI recognizes the dichotomy that parents struggle with as their children grow up and leave home. I'll let the artificial wisdom of my chatbot speak for itself.

Excitement bubbles up, like a fizzy soda escaping its confines. The nest, once bustling with youthful chirps and flapping wings, now awaits a different rhythm. The echoes of laughter will fade, replaced by the gentle hum of solitude.

Empty rooms, once cluttered with toys and dreams, now stretch their arms wide, yearning for purpose. The kitchen table, once a canvas for crayon masterpieces, will host quiet dinners for two. The front door, once a gateway to adventures, now stands still, awaiting the return of grown-up footsteps.

Freedom tiptoes in, wearing the shoes of nostalgia. The house exhales, releasing memories like dandelion seeds carried by the wind. Parents, with a mix of pride and wistfulness, watch their fledglings soar into the vast sky of independence.

And as the last car disappears around the corner, the house settles into a new chapter. The silence, once feared, becomes a companion. The walls, adorned with family portraits, whisper stories of love and growth.

Excited for kids to leave home? Yes, but also tenderly aware that their absence is a testament to a job well done. The nest may be empty, but the heart remains full.

The heart remains full. And the heart can be full of love and anticipation and hope as well as sorrow and fear and uncertainty. It's fascinating how we can feel so many emotions at once. And it's a testament to our resilience that we can bounce back from struggles, adapt to changes, and keep moving forward. Resilience is built one step at a time, just as launching our children is done one step at a time. Let's do this! Let's do it well!

How's Your Heart?

1. Do you feel prepared to launch your children into adulthood?

2. What emotions have you experienced as you watch your children become young adults?

3. What do you feel are your greatest needs in this season of life? What are the greatest needs of your children?

4. Do you feel resilient in this season of life? What would it take for you to feel more resilient?

Embrace Truth

Lord, Give me strength to put all of my faith and trust in your perfect plan and light my way with your truth. May my actions reflect your grace, my heart proclaim your glory, and my life be an echo of your love. Remind me of your promises when I'm doubting, and envelop me in your peace when I'm struggling. Let my life be an example of complete surrender to your will, Amen.

Do not be anxious about anything, but in every situation, by prayer and petition, with thanksgiving, present your requests to God. And the peace of God, which transcends all understanding, will guard your hearts and your minds in Christ Jesus.
Philippians 4:6-7

And those who know your name put their trust in you, for you, O Lord, have not forsaken those who seek you.
Psalm 9:10

2

GRIEF IS AN EXPRESSION OF LOVE

No one ever told me that grief feels so much like fear.
C.S. Lewis

Many moms grieve the changing stages of childhood, especially when their children become teenagers and near young adulthood. And change is hard, even when it is positive change. Moms may begin to feel unneeded, or like they have been demoted. There is a sense that their role in their children's lives has diminished as they become more independent. But the truth is, our roles as moms doesn't diminish, it evolves. Just as our children cycle in and out of seasons of childhood, so must our roles as moms evolve along with them. This is in line with the stages of parenting. (More on this in the next chapter.) What is it that we feel we are losing when our children grow up? For many moms, it is purpose or control. And losing purpose or control can create fear.

A GOOD THING

I began to grieve my daughter growing up during her senior year of high school. Life seemed to be moving at a rapid pace, and I knew the year would be over in the blink of an eye. I often thought in terms of her last—last high school dance, last spring break, last sleepover, last spontaneous girl's day out. It wasn't until she voiced how much this bothered her that I realized I was even doing it. I realized I had a doom-and-gloom outlook instead of one of anticipation. My heart was so heavy with what I thought I was losing that I couldn't see all the good things happening around me. My daughter's sharing helped me change my perspective from sad sentimentality to excited anticipation. I began looking forward to shopping for her college apartment, meeting her new friends, discussing what classes she would take, and what we would do as a family to capture fun moments together while we could.

But that's not to say I still didn't grieve the changing seasons of life we were all experiencing; I just wasn't as vocal about it with her. My sadness about what I thought I was losing was robbing her of the joy of an exciting future. Over a decade ago, one mom wrote this, and it still holds true: "The most crucial thing of all is to never pass the weight of your own grief on to your child. It is absolutely fine to tell them that you miss them, or that you will be sad when they leave. But you cannot make them bear the responsibility for your own sadness and pain. It may be tempting to ask your child to stay, or cry because they are leaving you, but that will only compromise the possibility of them finding happiness and independence."[1]

I took my heavy heart to the Lord more often, and he helped transform my perspective. I realized I wasn't losing her; she was just becoming the mature, responsible, independent young adult I had raised her to become. As another mom put it, "They're changing and growing away from us every day. And it's true that this, in itself, is a wonderful thing. It is a *good* thing."[2] Looking for the positives helps minimize the pain and shifts our grief into joy one day at a time.

TAKE TIME TO GRIEVE

The weight of grief you experience when your child becomes a young adult may surprise you, but acknowledging its depth is the key to healing. This season of grief is often downplayed because, after all, isn't your child becoming an independent adult the goal? So, the advice is often to stay busy and not think about it. But healing isn't found in avoidance. And we can't heal on the run. It's common to hear people talk about keeping busy so they can avoid the pain, but it doesn't work long term. It will resurface. It will come out in an unhealthy way if we don't deal with it in a healthy way. We must sit and mourn. Allowing ourselves to feel the hurt and acknowledging how we are is an important step in grieving and eventually moving into the next season of life.

My morning routine as a mom is to go for a run and then have quiet time in prayer and reading the Bible before I start my day. It was during that time that I would ask the Lord to help me surrender for the day, to carry my grief and help me heal, to help me accept the new normal for our family. And then I found things to be grateful for in the season of life I found myself.

I was grateful my son had such a solid group of friends who were unashamed of their faith. I was proud of his ambition and success in school and rock climbing and his servant's heart that had him volunteering in the first-grade class at church. And I was grateful my daughter was confident and showing independence. I was grateful she had good friends, would be attending college in-state, and that our relationship was in a good place. I was thankful she loved Jesus and had a heart to serve others.

After my daughter was in college, the hardest part of the day for me was first thing in the morning and just before bed. I missed getting to see her face in the morning and giving her a hug. And I missed getting to reconnect with her at the end of the day and telling her goodnight. Honestly, it was the little interactions I missed the most—just getting to see her face throughout the day. It would hit me at random times. I'd often go into her room and look at her childhood belongings that didn't make the cut for the college dorm, and I would let the tears fall. I'd say a prayer for her—for protection, new friends, fun experiences, meaningful classes—and I'd ask the Lord to help me surrender her into his hands. I would lift my hands and open them as a physical sign of the surrender that was so difficult to do. And I would often repeat that gesture throughout the day as a reminder of the new normal we were all living.

One mom wrote, "Grief feels too heavy of a word to use for this situation, one where I am also feeling pride and joy and hope. I was thrilled that my daughters were acclimating so well and a little guilty that I was so sad they were gone. I just felt off." Then she described the term *momancholy*— it's grief and gratitude, joy and heartbreak, love and sorrow.[3] Grief can and will encompass all of those feelings.

Talking with my husband and friends who understood what I was going through was a huge help. Sharing with someone who understands and encourages you through difficult seasons can ease the pain and help you navigate the grief well. The most important thing is to allow the grief process to unfold naturally and not deny what you are feeling. There were days I felt like I wouldn't survive, finding it difficult to take the next step, but other times I felt I had come a long way and was getting past the grief. It is not linear. Grief comes and goes at will. It is triggered by seemingly random things at random times. It is a demanding companion that won't go away if we ignore it. Grief is something we must walk through for as long as it takes. As the late Rev. Billy Graham once said, "Grief is like going through a tunnel—and sometimes we wonder if we'll ever come out the other end. But God has not abandoned you, and he wants to comfort you and assure you that he is with you. Jesus' words are true: 'Blessed are those who mourn, for they will be comforted.'"[4] God sees your hurting heart and is "the Father of compassion and the God of all comfort, who comforts us in all our troubles."[5]

EMBRACE A NEW NORMAL

Change is loss. And we can't let go and move on until we deal with the pain of loss. And our children becoming adults is a loss—loss of childhood, loss of family as we know it, loss of time with our children, loss of our mom role as we know it. We aren't losing our children; we are still their moms, but we are losing what we considered the norm for the past eighteen-plus years. Confronting the pain by grieving well is the first step in moving forward into a new season of life. The first thing we have to do is admit there is a new normal.

It's normal to long for things to be the way they were, but it is counterproductive. Things will not go back to the way they were; our young adult children will not become children again. We have to be honest and admit there is a new normal. And it's one in which we won't have control. Our children becoming young adults means letting them make their own choices. It means letting them succeed and fail on their own. It means letting them choose how much time they spend with us. It means empowering them. And it means holding our tongues more often than not.

Being a mom to a young adult means letting your role as a mom shift, embracing a new type of relationship, and finding new (or old) activities to fill your time. Dust off those running shoes you haven't used in years. Ask friends to join you for an exercise class. Or take a cooking class. Plan regular date nights with your husband. Schedule fun activities to do with your children still at home. Learn an instrument. Take up dancing. As you find more time on your hands with your young adult child out of the house, find fun ways to fill it.

The day-to-day reality of having a child who is no longer living at home is hard. You will inevitably learn less about their lives, including where they are and what they are doing with their time. It's important to communicate with your child; while you should give them room to grow up and enjoy their new life, it's also healthy to check in with them.

Let your young adult set the pace for communication. When my daughter went to college, I worried about how often we would talk or text. I didn't want to harness her with expectations like, "Call us every Sunday night." I wanted her to have the freedom of Sunday evening ice cream runs with friends or playing games with roommates after a spontaneous invitation. I never wanted her to feel an obligation to home that would interfere with her homework, making new friends, or embracing a new social life. As it turns out, I need not worry. She would text me at least once a day, often much more, telling me about a class, a new friend, or an opportunity. When she had more time, she would call and we would talk longer. She wanted to be in touch with me. And I found that it felt easier to reach out to her when there was something I wanted to share with her.

I know this won't be the case with every child. I often wonder what it will be like when my son goes to college. As it is, he doesn't talk on the phone much. He texts very short responses when I need to reach out and ask him something. (This is the way of many boys, right?) The point is, there isn't a set formula. If you aren't hearing from your young adult child as much as you'd like, have a conversation with him about it. Maybe you could agree to catch up once a week over a phone call when it is convenient for him. Try establishing communication with fun texts, a reminder of her that made you laugh, a meme that you knew he'd enjoy, or a funny story about something that happened to you at the store. Model the type of relationship you want to have with them. You just might be surprised at how responsive they are to no-strings-attached communication. Instead of a barrage of questions, show them you want to communicate like you do with your friends.

A new normal will look different for everyone. But we have to make it easy for our children to say yes to our invitations, and we have to make it easy for them to say no—without guilt —which means not voicing our hurts, concerns, or desires in response to their choices. A new normal might be that your young adult child

- is no longer present for dinner every night,
- doesn't attend the same church as you (or go at all),
- comes home later than you want them to,
- spends more time with friends than family,
- doesn't ask your advice as often (or at all), and
- doesn't call or text regularly.

Don't fret over the new normal. Chances are, it will shift as your young adult children learn to live in their new season of life. They are trying on new identities and figuring out who they are apart from Mom and Dad. Sometimes they may make choices that push the limits just because they can. Let it be okay. Be there to encourage them, support them, and offer suggestions *if they ask*. A big part of our new normal as parents of young adults is being present and listening but not telling them what to do, or saying, "I told you so!" when things don't go the way they thought they would.

In this season of life, as my children are growing into young adults and venturing out on their own, I have been surprised by grief because I didn't see it coming; it's the part of parenting no one seems to talk about. Surely, if I was happy to see my children thriving, I wouldn't feel sad about it. But over the past few years, I have learned a lot about grief. Primarily, that grief is an expression of love.

That's why psychologists call it a silver lining: "In times of loss, when grief seems all-consuming, it's crucial to remember that grief is, in essence, a manifestation of love. The two are inseparably intertwined, and to grieve is to love. By reframing our perspective and [recognizing] the depth of love that our grief signifies, we can find strength, solace, and, eventually, a path to healing. Let us [honor] our grief, for it is the clearest sign that we have loved deeply and truly."[6]

When we grieve, it's because we have loved. It is the price we pay for caring so profoundly about another person. And I wonder, is there any deeper love than a mother for her child?

How's Your Heart?

1. Have you experienced grief in this season of life? How have you processed it?

2. How can you shift your perspective to experience joy in this season of life?

3. What does your new normal look like? Take time to articulate it by writing it down.

4. How can you honor your grief in this season of life?

Embrace Truth

Lord, My heart is sad, and I don't know what to do but come to you right now. Help me process what I am going through and not sweep my feelings under the rug. Be with me every moment I am going through this. Enable me to fix my eyes on you and cling to you during this time. Thank you, that you meet me right where I am, Amen.

My flesh and my heart may fail, but God is the strength of my heart and my portion forever.
Psalm 73:26

The LORD is near to the brokenhearted and saves the crushed in spirit.
Psalm 34:18

3

A JOURNEY OF STAGES

Teenagers are a work in progress, but so are parents.
Barbara Colorosa

Parenting teenagers and young adult children is a delicate balance of letting go and staying connected. Our hearts sway between release and connection, and the temptation is to tighten our grips. But if love is proved in letting go (as C Day-Lewis so bravely penned—see opening quote of Chapter 1), why do we rage so hard against it when the time comes? Perhaps the catalyst we need is a shift in perspective to align with our shifting roles as moms.

The stages of parenting came on the scene in the 1980s when Ellen Galinsky recognized the development of parents and looked at how they grow as their children grow. She identified six stages of parenting,[1] the last two being the Interdependent Stage (adolescence) and the Departure Stage (early adulthood).

Then in 2007, Bob Hostetler of Focus on the Family wrote about the four stages of parenting: Commander, Coach, Counselor, and Consultant. The last two, Counselor and Consultant, align with Galinsky's Interdependent and Departure stages. I want to focus on these last two stages because it is in these stages that our children transition into adulthood.

COUNSELOR STAGE (INTERDEPENDENT)

In this stage of parenting, our children need guidance. It's here that we must redefine our authority and renegotiate our relationship with our adolescents. We don't give them complete autonomy, but we allow them to make more decisions independent of parental control and authority.

"Too many of us continue to parent our teenagers in much the same way we parented them as toddlers or grade-schoolers. When our kids begin to strain against the reins, like a horse that's eager to run, we pull back hard—as though it's wrong for them to seek independence. But that's exactly the purpose of the teen years. In fact, we should encourage that drive for independence and channel it in the right direction," wrote Hostetler. He encouraged parents to use the phrase, "That's a decision *you* can make."[2] Encourage them to take responsibility in making decisions, offer suggestions, and warn of potential consequences of poor decisions, but leave the decision in your adolescent's hands. The risk is that they might make a bad decision, and sometimes they will. But over time they will learn to make the right decisions as we empower them to think for themselves. It takes practice, and that's the primary responsibility of parents in this stage—let them practice making decisions. Consider it a low-control, high-accountability stage.

As a freshman in high school, my son had been rock climbing competitively for several years. He spent most of his free time at the climbing gym, either for team practices or climbing with friends for fun. So, when he came home one day and said the gym owner wanted to hire him to help coach the younger team, we weren't surprised. He had been demonstrating strong leadership skills at school and church, and it no doubt translated to his team experience. He asked me and his dad what he should do, and we responded, "You get to decide." We talked through his school schedule and homework load and how much free time that would leave him. We discussed his commitment to the climbing team and whether it would be too much to work at the gym. And ultimately, he decided it would be a fun way to make some extra money, doing something he loves.

My husband and I gave our son complete control over his decision to work, but we still held him to the standards of completing his homework on time and doing it well. He rose to the occasion and thrived with his new schedule and responsibility. We not only encouraged critical thinking, we empowered him to make a big decision on his own, and we supported his decision and affirmed his process in concluding that he could handle working part-time while in high school. This stage of parenting is a great opportunity for growth—for teens and parents alike.

CONSULTANT STAGE (DEPARTURE)

It's in this stage that parents assess their accomplishments and failures. It begins the transition into a new era for parents. "The task of parenting isn't done at this stage; it is no longer one of proactive involvement but of patient availability," according to Hostetler. The operative phrase for this stage of parenting is, "Let me know if I can help."[3] This affirms our availability as moms but respects our young adult children's independence. The primary responsibility of parents in this stage is support. It's in this stage of life that our children need space to become the adults we raised them to be. It's in this stage that parents practice active listening, encourage critical thinking, and share wisdom when it is asked for. This is where friendship with our adult children begins and grows.

I fully practiced this stage of parenting when, a few weeks before Christmas, our daughter was rear-ended in a snow storm. She was okay, but her car sustained significant damage.

Initially, I handled some of the logistics for her. But as it became overwhelming for me with my full schedule, I realized it was an opportunity for her to adult and learn how to navigate a difficult situation. She filed the police report, called the insurance company, and setup an appointment with the chiropractor to be assessed for whiplash. Over the next several months, she fielded all the calls with insurance companies and the rental car company. There were setbacks and delays, but I saw her rise to the occasion and handle them with confidence. Several times she would ask me or her dad for advice, but she used her voice to get what she needed.

Once she got her car back from the repair shop, she decided she wanted to sell it and buy something newer and more reliable. And that is where I saw her shine as a young adult. From beginning to end of the car-buying process, she navigated it on her own. She researched cars, scheduled test drives, negotiated with salesmen, and, ultimately, bought her new car on her own, driving a hard bargain so that she came in under budget!

PRACTICE WHAT WE PREACH

These shifting stages of parenting can be difficult to discern, but it serves us and our growing young adult children well to stop treating them as if they are still the children we wish they were. Our children outgrow us much sooner than we outgrow them. It's not their fault that we aren't ready for them to grow up, but it is our responsibility to let it happen and foster their transition with grace, love, and support. As one dad so aptly said, "It is one thing to show your child the way, and a harder thing to then stand out of it."[4]

Releasing our children to become young adults isn't easy. There's no formula, and it takes practice and renewed commitment to doing it well, often on a daily basis. But here are a few tips from A Modern Midlife that might help you along the way. [5]

- Realize and accept that your relationship is changing.
  Your relationship is changing from parent-child to adult-adult. You will always be their mom, but now you get to be their friend.

- Give them space to be independent.
  Let it be up to them how much they call on you for guidance and assistance. Don't hover; allow them space to do their own things.

- Let them make mistakes.
  Show your children you believe in them by letting them make their own decisions and fail when necessary. This is how we all learn.

- Let go of your interpretation of success.
  Your dreams for your children's lives may not match their dreams. Success may look different to them, and that's okay. We are not responsible for our children's success as adults.

- Understand that you're not losing them.
  Your relationship will be different, but you are not losing them. You will always be their mom even when their lives do not revolve around you. You're no longer in control but are now a friend who offers support.

I love how the Scary Mommy blog wrote about our children growing up being the best and worst thing: "When you witness your child making discoveries about themselves and the world, when you literally watch them becoming an adult before your eyes, your heart all but bursts with joy and gratitude. But the truth is that a bursting heart feels an awful lot like a breaking one. The joy and the pain both pummel you harder than you expect them to. You think by now you should be used to this kind of emotional upheaval as your kids grow and change, but it never gets easier. There's nothing greater than watching your child walk toward their wide-open future, and nothing worse than watching them walk away from you."[6]

One dad put it this way, "Children arrive, they take over your life and then, one day, they walk off with it."[7] And isn't that what it feels like? That they are walking away from us as they walk toward their future? That they took our life with them? It's an accurate and troubling juxtaposition and one that isn't complete. Our adult children do leave, as they should, physically and emotionally, but that doesn't mean they are leaving the relationship. They go off on their own, to college or a first apartment. They find jobs, new friends, and new places to spend their time. They make choices about money, faith, politics, how to spend their time, where to live, who to date and eventually marry, and where to set boundaries. They are the new gate keepers of their lives, which often feels like there's little to no room for Mom or Dad or siblings. Ultimately, they get to decide. It's as it should be. But I truly believe if they have felt supported, loved, encouraged, and cared for well during those transitional years, they will make an effort to maintain a relationship with their family.

Our daughter had plans to move in with a friend after her college graduation, but it fell through at the last minute. She was heartbroken and at a loss for what to do next. After weeks of praying, talking, and listening, she decided to live at home. It was not what she wanted at the time, but she valued the time she would have with her family since she would be getting married in a couple of years. I was heartbroken for her for the loss of her dream, but I was thankful for more time with her on a daily basis. As she talked about what this new normal would look like, she said, "I feel like a little kid. I'm still living in the room we decorated when I was in middle school." I was taken aback; she was a new college graduate at the age of nineteen, but it felt like it had only been a couple of years since we had updated her room. I didn't even hesitate to tell her that I would help her redecorate her room. We painted, set up the "adult" furniture she had in storage for her apartment, hung new curtains and pictures, and boxed up all the little girl things that she no longer wanted on display in her room.

Then we talked about new boundaries. She was a college graduate with a remote job that allowed her to work from home. Her dad and I helped her set up an office area and reiterated that she was an adult and did not need our permission to do things; she could come and go as she wanted. (I only asked for the courtesy of knowing if she would be home in the evenings so I could plan dinner accordingly.) I consciously chose to not rely on her to help with her younger brother regularly. Occasionally, I would ask her to give him a ride if I had a conflict. But it was the exception instead of the norm, and it was never her problem to solve if it didn't work for her schedule.

And the coolest thing happened. My daughter made family time a priority without me asking. She was conscious of how much she was gone during the week and made sure to have time at home at least once or twice a week. She would take her lunch break at the same time as her brother so they could hang out. She would schedule breakfast dates with her dad and ask me to go shopping or get a pedicure with her. As a young adult, she modeled the same values and priorities she had been raised with—family, friends, and faith.

But what happens if our adult children don't model the same values and priorities we raised them with? Biting our tongue is a big part of parenting adult children. And just like we had to choose our battles when they were young, we have to choose carefully when we *don't* hold our tongue. As young adults, they want and need autonomy. They are a separate person with opinions and ideas, and they have a right to exercise making their own decisions. It's about proving to their parents that they can handle adulthood without us.

Dr. Laurence Steinberg, author of *You and Your Adult Child,* suggests not offering advice unless it is asked for or you see your adult child about to make a harmful, dangerous, irrevocable decision. Unsolicited advice has a way of making our young adult children question themselves. A friend saying the same thing wouldn't have the same effect, but when a parent says something, it can make our young adult children question their maturity and competence.[8] For example, if your son is looking at an apartment and you say, "Do you really want to live here next to a noisy restaurant? Will you be able to sleep?" He might wonder why he didn't think of that himself and question whether he is even asking the right questions. It behooves us to ask questions instead of just saying what we think, which is a round-about way to offer advice — "What do you think of a restaurant being next door?"

ALMOST NOT YET

One day when my daughter was twelve years old, she had an uncharacteristic outburst while discussing something with her dad. I don't remember the particulars, but I remember her shouting, "I'm twelve years old! I'm not a kid!" as she fled from the room. My husband and I stood in shocked silence, as we had never seen such an emotional outburst from our happy-go-lucky little girl. My husband asked, "What just happened?" I was just as confused as he was. About ten minutes later, he found her sitting on the porch crying. He sat by her in silence, waiting for her to talk. (He's always been good at this with both of our children. His presence conveys, "I'm here when you are ready to talk.") She eventually whispered through her tears, "Dad, I am *only* twelve years old."

This story illustrates the tension that exists for our children in the "almost/not yet" chasm that builds in the teenage years and continues into young adulthood. They want to be treated as adults, but they aren't fully adults yet. So, what do we do as parents? What if we gave them more responsibility and see if they rise to the occasion? What if we are there to help them navigate decisions when the consequences are small?

As our children near adulthood, we can encourage responsibility and help them build confidence by how we interact with them. Insisting they are still children when they long for independence can stifle growth. There is no harm in giving our children autonomy as they grow into young adults. After all, while they are still living at home, it gives us a chance to navigate how they will handle their new-found freedom and responsibilities. And we can converse with them about their decisions and the outcomes that follow.

How's Your Heart?

1. Were you familiar with the stages of parenting? Which stage have you found to be the hardest?

2. Do you find shifting into the next stage of parenting easy or difficult?

3. Which of the tips for releasing your children is the most challenging for you?

4. Is there a circumstance right now where you can let your young adult child make the decisions? How can you enable them to choose wisely?

Embrace Truth

Lord, I love you and want to know you more and more. I long for an increasingly intimate relationship with you. Help me cultivate spiritual disciplines and spend more time in worshipful listening. Remind me that you are always with me and give me courage for the road ahead, Amen.

Be strong and courageous. Do not be frightened, and do not be dismayed, for the LORD your God is with you wherever you go.
Joshua 1:9

He must increase, but I must decrease.
John 3:30

4

TRUST ISN'T BLIND FAITH

Children need models rather than critics.
Joseph Joubert

"Parenting is about raising and celebrating the child you have, not the child you thought you would have." What wise words from *The Water Giver: The Story of a Mother, a Son, and Their Second Chance!*[1] We are raising our children to be their best selves, not who we want them to be. We are raising them to change the culture, not conform to it. It's worth noting that the author of *The Water Giver* went on to say, "It's about understanding that he is exactly the person he is supposed to be. And, if you're lucky, he just might be the teacher who turns you into the person you're supposed to be."[2] I love that—our children as our teachers!

C. Dwight Bain who calls himself a Change Coach (I'm pretty sure I need one!) gave this advice about launching our children into adulthood: "As hard as it may be for parents to consider letting go of the children they have invested so much time and energy into, it is essential for the child's healthy development and inner strength as a confident person who will one day have to move out and move on. Young adults need the skill to tackle issues directly throughout their lives without the security of knowing that Mom and Dad's watchful care is always going to be near. Or that Mom or Dad will be there to rescue them after every wrong decision. The goal is for children to know what they believe, and when tested, to pass the test and live out those beliefs despite the pressures around them."[3]

FOR OR TO?

I often joke, "We raise our kids to be strong, confident, independent, contributing members of society, and then, dang it, they do it!" To me, that statement captures the tension between being proud of who my children are becoming and the sadness of seeing them go (or perhaps need me less). I've never heard a parent say, "I'm raising my kids to remain dependent on me and live in my house forever and never forge their own path." Of course not. So, why is it that when it is time for our young adult children to venture out into the world on their own, we tend to buckle down and tighten our grip? Why do we sometimes act as if they are doing something wrong and believe we have to step in and stop them from going any further? Could it be that we have lost sight of (or never even considered) what we are raising our children for? Or better yet, what are we raising our children *to*?

Our twenty-one-year-old daughter, who is engaged to be married, is living at home and working remotely in a full-time job. As she occasionally does, she told me and her dad one day that she would be traveling that week to visit her fiancé at college. It's something we have always supported as we know from experience how difficult long-distance relationships can be. She has friends to stay with, money to pay for her own gas, and the ability to work from anywhere. We didn't question her choice. My husband later expressed his warring emotions over our daughter announcing she was going on a trip—not asking permission but telling—and how weird it felt to see her doing these grown-up things. That's how we raised her, and we had set that new boundary when she turned eighteen and we considered her an adult. She was doing exactly what we had raised her to do—be an adult. It was then that the question popped into my mind: What are we raising our children for?

Are we not raising them to launch them? Launching our kids well doesn't begin when they leave home; it begins when they are young. When we empower them to make choices; when we encourage them to try new things; when we comfort them in their failures; when we discipline their misdeeds; when we teach them how to wash dishes and do laundry and put gas in the car; when we show them that having fun matters just as much as working hard; when we apologize and take responsibility and forgive easily and refuse to cast blame. This is all preparation for the day they leave home and begin to live as young adults in the world.

Will they do it perfectly? Of course not. Will we? No way! But we can keep our ultimate goal in mind—to launch our children well to the life God has called them to. We aren't raising our children to fulfill our dreams or follow the course we have mapped out for them. We are raising them to be the people God created them to be. We are raising them to holiness, honesty, and kindness. We are raising them to confidence. We are raising them to love well and to every high value we esteem within our own families. What are those values within your family and home? Are your children aware of those values? Do you talk about them openly and often?

As a pastor, my brother has three profoundly deep and simple core values for his family, based on John Mark Comer's framework in his book *Practicing the Way*—Be with Jesus. Become like him. Do as he did. He explained it to me this way, "In our ministry, we use the mantra 'Belong. Believe. Become.' The more we spend time with Jesus, the more we become like Jesus, which will naturally lead to doing things the way he did them and doing the kinds of things he did."

When my children were little, I typed out our family's core values and had them framed. By the time they were teenagers, they knew the core values that defined our family by heart. They knew them so well that I had a simple mantra I would repeat to them, and they knew exactly what it meant. I still say it to this day (and we often get a good laugh when they say it back to me). "Remember who you are. Remember whose you are." The point is that launching our children well is a process that begins in childhood. But it is never too late to choose to do it well. Our young adult children will launch into adulthood whether we are ready or not, and they will do it with our influence — be it positive or negative, healthy or unhealthy.

When our young adult children are graduating high school, going off to college, getting jobs, and forging their own lives, we have an opportunity as moms to foster a new adult relationship with them. I try to never forget that it is our ongoing relationship that is at stake. I don't have to agree with every decision they make. What matters is that my young adult children feel loved and supported. And yes, we can love and support our children even when we don't agree with their decisions. We have to keep in mind, we raised them to make their own decisions. We raised them to face the world and choose their path even if it differs from our own. Because we trust God with them. We trust he is in control and that he is working in their lives. It is that trust that allows us to loosen our grips and ultimately surrender.

LEARNING TO TRUST

Every single day of our lives was determined before we took our first breath. God knew us before we were formed in the womb. What a humbling revelation to know God has full control of our lives. "All the days ordained for me were written in your book before one of them came to be," said the psalmist David in Psalm 139. And God said to Jeremiah, "Before I formed you in the womb I knew you, before you were born I set you apart; I appointed you as a prophet before the nations" (1:5). *Before* he was born he was appointed? God has a calling on each of our lives that he ordained long before we were created. And our expectations for our young adult children may not match their calling.

As moms, part of our calling is raising the children he has entrusted into our care. But we don't do so blindly. It's often said there are no instructions for being a parent. In one sense that is true. But we do have God's Word, and we have the assurance that he planned their lives and their calling and ordained their days just as he did for us. Do we trust the plans he has for our children? And if we do, can we surrender the control that has us holding so tightly to them as they grow? Especially as they transition into young adults?

In an article titled, "Parenting Is a Progressive Letting Go," Anna Meade Harris described why it can feel easier to hold on than let go as our children become young adults. "At every age and stage, our children's maturation demands that we let them grow up. We launch them gradually into the world: to school, to spend the night at a friend's house, to drive a car, to college, and so on. Bit by bit, we step back and let them make their own choices, praying that they will listen closely for God's voice. Perhaps the trickiest part is knowing *when* and *how* to let them take the reins of their own lives. It often feels easier to maintain control rather than run the risk of our child making a poor decision."[4]

As moms, we need to trust God is protecting our children. He gives us children as a gift, on loan to raise, nurture, and love forward into adulthood. It's hard—much harder than we realize it will be. But we let go in faith. We pray and trust God to protect and guide our children just as he does with us. Letting go allows our children to develop their own faith muscles. It's a tremendous faith workout for moms, but as we release our children into his care, he matures us and deepens our faith. And he does the same for our children.

In his book *Our Greatest Gift*, Henri Nouwen tells this story about the Flying Rodleighs, trapeze artists whom he befriended:

> One day, I was sitting with Rodleigh, the leader of the troupe, in his caravan, taking about flying. He said, "As a flyer, I must have complete trust in my catcher. The public might think that I am the great star of the trapeze, but the real star is Joe, my catcher. He has to be there for me with split-second precision and grab me out of the air as I come to him in the long jump."
>
> "How does it work?" I asked. "The secret," Rodleigh said, "is that the flyer does nothing and the catcher does everything. When I fly to Joe, I have simply to stretch out my arms and wait for him to catch me and pull me safely over the apron behind the catchbar."
>
> "You do nothing!" I said, surprised. "Nothing," Rodleigh repeated. "The worst thing the flyer can do is try to catch the catcher. I am not supposed to catch Joe. It's Joe's task to catch me. If I grabbed Joe's wrists, I might break them, or he might break mine, and it would be the end for both of us. A flyer must fly, and a catcher must catch, and the flyer must trust, with outstretched arms, that his catcher will be there for him."

Is this not the job of parents raising children into adulthood —to trust, learn to let go, and allow them to fly? We've given them roots; now we need to give them wings.

Just as the flyer must resist the temptation to help the catcher by grabbing him, we have to resist the temptation to play God with our children. We have to be willing to let them fail. (Aren't our greatest times of growth rooted in our biggest failures? Let's not rob our children of these God-appointed opportunities.) It is uncomfortable and scary at times, but it's a sign of growth for us as moms. It goes against our protective instincts to release control of our child's choices, and it is even more counterintuitive not to snatch control back when we are afraid. Ultimately, we cling tightly to our kids not only for their sake but for ours as well. We try to avoid our own pain by preventing theirs, yet we sacrifice growth, maturity, and thriving for our whole family when we are unwilling to trust God with our children. We are the flyer. God is the catcher. Let him catch you; let him catch your children.

God has proven himself trustworthy since the beginning of time, but we are quick to trust many things—ourselves included—over God. This is the struggle for perceived control. It doesn't matter if they are headed for kindergarten or college, when our children walk out the front door, God is the only one who can go with them. And God is the only one with the power to catch them, hold them, and bring them safely home.

WHO IS THE HOLY SPIRIT?

I often tell my children, "I'm not your Holy Spirit." As much as I want to be at times, I have to stop myself from trying to control their choices when I should be empowering them to flex their decision-making muscles. It does not serve them well if I make all of their decisions for them. Letting go means doing so in faith. We pray, talk to more experienced parents, and examine our young adult children as individuals who are no longer an extension of us. This letting go means trusting God to catch our children when they need it—in his perfect timing.

The story of the prodigal son in Luke 15 is a perfect example of this teaching. When his younger son demanded his inheritance, the father knew his beloved son would head straight for a far country to squander his inheritance on reckless living (v. 13). His son was an adult. His dad had known him all of his life, and he knew exactly what his son would do with the money and his freedom. But the father was willing to endure great sadness and anguish, trusting his son would remember who his father was and who he was before he strayed.

When my daughter was nineteen years old, she and her boyfriend sat down with me and her dad and told us they were thinking about getting engaged. It did not come as a surprise to us; they had been dating since they were sixteen, and we knew they were serious. What did come as a surprise is that they wanted to get married right after she graduated the following year. They would both be twenty years old, and he would still have two years of college to finish. It didn't feel like they were rushing—they had been in a relationship for three years at that point—but it felt like my daughter's life was on fast forward. She had finished high school a semester early and graduated college in two years—all before the age of twenty. I was barely getting used to her living away from home and being in college when graduation was upon us, and she was looking to the next season of life.

Her dad and I were grateful they invited us into the conversation of their engagement. They weren't asking for permission; they were seeking guidance. We told them we would pray about it with them and asked them to be open to the Holy Spirit's leading, even if it meant hearing they should wait. We asked them to seek other godly counsel and to take a premarital course while they were processing the pros and cons of engagement at such a young age. They agreed and in turn asked us to be open to the Holy Spirit, too, even if it meant they should proceed with getting married immediately after her graduation. I put on my "outward mom face" (more on this in chapter 5) and agreed. I was already praying for the Lord's wisdom and guidance as I panicked. I wasn't panicking because they wanted to get married, I truly believe they are meant to get married. I was panicking because I wasn't ready to enter that next (very adult) season of life with our not-so-little girl.

Over the next six months, the two of them prayed, met with mentors, and took a premarital course with trusted friends of ours. We would check in with them periodically and get updates, and they would share how they were growing and hearing from God. At some point, as they both readied to return to college—our daughter for her final year—they shared that the Holy Spirit had spoken to them and they were in agreement about waiting to get married. This is what happens when we trust the Holy Spirit to speak to our children—he does so in his timing. It's not that he answered the way I wanted him to; it's that I knew my daughter and her boyfriend were serious about seeking the Lord's will, and that he would faithfully answer in due time. Had he given them the green light to go ahead and get married, I would have supported their decision. It would have taken much more prayer and processing, but I believe the Lord would have given me peace either way.

As moms, we must remember who our children's Father is. God will speak directly to them without any help from us. They have the Holy Spirit just like we do, and he is responsible for sanctifying our children, not us. Our role is to teach them the truth of the Bible, but it is up to them to obey it. And when they do, it's not because we coerced their obedience or made their choices for them, it's because they have their own relationship with God. God is responsible for "catching" our children. It is up to us to disciple them well, then trust God, let them go, and let them fly.

One friend shared the story of her daughter's engagement after college and how she saw red flags but didn't say anything. She "prayed without ceasing" and decided to trust the Holy Spirit to intervene if the marriage was not God's will. And he did; eventually, her daughter broke off the engagement because of the same red flags. In the weeks and months of grief that followed, this mom had many conversations with her daughter about hearing from the Holy Spirit. It's what she called a "near miss" but the Holy Spirit "caught" her daughter in the aftermath of a difficult change of heart. Several years would pass before God brought the right man into her life.

Another friend shared the story of her teenage daughter rebelling in high school. She seemingly had turned her back on the faith she was raised with despite the constant prayers of her parents. She went away to college and returned with a baby on the way. Her parents were heartbroken, but God …

He was already in the process of redeeming her story although they would not see the fruit of it for years to come. This is the power of intercessory prayer.

God's faithfulness does not depend on us. Our children will make poor choices at times, but it is not up to us to control their choices or manipulate their futures. We cannot "catch" ourselves, so we have learned to trust God with our own lives. How much more do we need to learn to trust him with the children we love so much? Is he not the ultimate "catcher"?

How's Your Heart?

1. Do you trust God with your children? It is easy to say yes, but do you live as if you truly trust him and his plan—especially if it is not the one you would write for your children?

2. What area of your child's life do you need to surrender to the Lord?

3. Do you talk to your children about the Holy Spirit and give him time and space to speak to them?

4. Have your children ever told you the Holy Spirit was leading them in a direction that you didn't want them to go? How did you handle it?

Embrace Truth

Lord, I come before you with a heart struggling for control. I cling to the reins of my life like a child clings to a toy, fearful of what might happen if I let go. But you invite me to let go and put my faith in your tender hands. Help me unclench my fists and cast my worries, plans, and sense of control at your feet. Clothe me in trust and peace as I surrender to you, Amen.

Trust in the LORD with all your heart
and lean not on your own understanding;
in all your ways submit to him,
and he will make your paths straight.
Proverbs 3:5-6

But blessed is the one who trusts in the Lord, whose confidence is in him.
Jeremiah 17:7

5

ADULTHOOD IS THE SCARIEST HOOD

Parenthood is one long exercise in relinquishing control,
or the illusion that we ever had it.
Jane Adams

When do our children become adults? I never thought about it until the time was upon us. My daughter was weeks from high school graduation and turning eighteen. She would move to a new city to attend college a few months after that. She had long since been very responsible and mature beyond her years. She volunteered regularly and worked odd jobs to make money. All signs of adulthood. But she wasn't financially independent; she still lived at home. My husband and I had spent years empowering her to make decisions and teaching her to think critically, logically, and for herself. We trusted her and gave her more freedom and responsibility as she grew. It was a way to gauge how she would handle those freedoms and responsibilities while still under our roof, so we could have conversations and guide her as needed before she was on her own.

One day a friend told me that when her daughter turned

eighteen, she and her husband told her she was an adult, no longer had a curfew, and didn't have to ask permission to do things anymore. For them, adulthood began at eighteen years old. It took me a few weeks of processing, but I began to feel that was an appropriate course to take with my daughter. After talking to my husband about it, we agreed that was the path we would take. It was a little scary for me as a mom, but my husband was supportive and always listened when I needed to verbally process. And the cool thing is we saw our daughter thrive. She didn't abuse her new adult status; she flourished in it. She told us where she would be and with whom (part of the agreement), but she didn't have to ask to do those things. By the time we dropped her off at college, we were confident she would do well in her new environment. Unlike many freshmen she encountered, she didn't stay out all night or skip class or party. She made responsible choices because she had already been doing it for so long.

Another friend said to me of her nearly twenty-one-year-old son, "He won't be an adult until he is financially independent." That was a new viewpoint for me, and it challenged me to consider what the signs of adulthood are. Surely, it's not just financial. What about living away from home? Or having a job? Or being a college graduate? Even if we continue to help them financially, does that negate their adulthood? Undoubtedly, economic dependence and emotional independence are tricky stages to navigate.

I decided to ask friends and family: When did you consider your children to be adults? The answers were all over the map. Some said when they graduated high school or turned eighteen. Others said when they moved out on their own, or when they had a full-time job. My dad told me it was when I figured out how to pay for college on my own. One lady, who I met in a very long line at the store, told me she didn't consider her daughter an adult until she got married at twenty-five. She had been living on her own before that but was making poor choices. It was the sign of responsibility in marriage that helped this mom see her daughter as an adult. And still, another dad echoed the sentiment that his college-age twins needed to be financially independent to be called adults. I suppose there is no one right answer.

I realized we don't all have to agree on when adulthood begins; it is perhaps an inchoate—undeveloped—target. But the thought came to me: What if we treated them like adults anyway? Even if we don't think they are adults yet, how would it benefit our teens and/or young adults to treat them like adults? Is that part of teaching them to be adults? And how do they become mature, responsible adults if we don't teach them?

As moms, we know how we want things done; we believe we know what's best for our children; we know we can spare them some hurt if they would just listen to us. But none of that is the point. The point of launching our children well is to empower them to make decisions. Not *good* decisions. Not *our* decisions. Not *right* decisions. We need to empower them to make decisions and teach them how to live with the consequences—good or bad.

All decisions have consequences (some good, some bad), and they have been learning this as they grow up. There must come a time when we let our children make more decisions as we make fewer decisions for them. This doesn't mean we don't offer guidance or advice (when asked), but we encourage them to think for themselves and choose. We praise them when it turns out well, and we comfort them when it doesn't. Every parent must find a way to release their children and recognize their passage into adulthood. It's difficult to do, but it is in the releasing that we find hope and peace. And the relationship begins to transform into a beautiful friendship. If we don't let our children experience failure, how will they learn?

Stanford's freshman dean for over a decade, Julie Lythcott-Haimes wrote a book on parenting that came out of her experience and the surprising and troubling trend she saw among students.

The worst part, unintended yet insidious, is this hidden message we send to kids: *I don't think you can do this without me.* Trying to boost them up, we are paradoxically tearing them down. We overhelp so as *not* to disadvantage them, yet they're disadvantaged *because* we do so much. *You're not good enough for this life as you are,* is the message. *You never will be. You need me. You will always need me.*

They didn't seem to know how to contend with what life would throw their way. How to sit with discomfort or indecision or opportunity and emerge with their own sense of how to move forward. So intertwined with their parents they didn't seem to know how to *be* their own selves.

Having the courage to be who we are regardless of what other people want us to be —*even parents*—is the path to a meaningful and rewarding life.[1]

CLEAR EXPECTATIONS

We may think our young adult children know what we expect of them, but those expectations should be clearly stated, not just implied, to avoid unnecessary misunderstandings or tension. Setting healthy boundaries can be awkward, but it's necessary. Becoming an adult is a process, and it's important to recognize that there are varying degrees of independence. Most young adults are emotionally independent before they are financially independent.

According to author Dr. Laurence Steinberg, it's never been more difficult for young adults to achieve financial independence than it is today. The most common living arrangement for young adults in their 20s is with their parents because it has become so difficult to establish their footing with the high prices of a turbulent economy. And it's important to note the difference between a young adult coming home from college on break and one moving back in after college or never leaving in the first place. Boundaries are a loving way to create a path toward responsibility for one's actions. Expressing expectations is a way of providing leadership for our children. We model the behavior we expect.

What are some healthy boundaries to consider for our young adult children? It will depend on the circumstances, whether they live at home or away at college and come home on breaks, or whether they have a full-time job but still live at home. But consider the following areas that will need healthy boundaries:

- Financial
  Do they pay rent if they live at home? Do you buy their groceries if they live at college? One dad told me his daughter was required to pay one-fifth of the mortgage while living at home after college because five people lived in the house. One mom said her son was allotted $100 per month for groceries while he was away at college.

- Communication
  How often do you talk? Is it better to text or call? Some friends of mine had a standing call with their son every Sunday night while he was away at college. Another friend said her daughter preferred email over text.

- Responsibilities
  Who makes their appointments, manages their finances, and handles their schedule? Once our daughter was working full-time, I empowered her to make her own appointments for the dentist, eye doctor, tire rotations, etc.

LETTING THEM BE SEPARATE

If parenthood is about relinquishing control, then post-parenthood[2] is about acceptance. It's normal for our teens to distance themselves from us. They are experimenting with independence. They have to discover who they will be as they step into the world as a healthy, independent adult. They aren't rejecting you; they are finding their own identity. It's a process that takes time; they will take risks and make choices we don't agree with. But the values we taught them are still there and will most likely resurface at some point as they mature.

The harder we fight to control them, the harder they will push against us. We need to make it easy for them to come to us when something happens or they need guidance. Ask questions more than you give advice. Give them information but don't lecture. Listen more than you talk. Fine-tune your listening skills and sharpen your questioning skills.

I learned those lessons when my daughter entered her tween years. And it was then that I perfected what I called the "outward mom face." This was the smiling, calm face my daughter saw when she told me something that caused me to panic on the inside. (It's important to note that, in hindsight, the vast majority of moments were not panic-worthy.) I didn't want my daughter to see alarm or concern, which I knew would shut down the conversation faster than it started. So, I would take a (covert) deep breath, smile, and say, "Tell me more about that." And she would. My daughter learned I was a safe place for her to share. She became an open book because I listened more than I talked, and I engaged with her on her level. When she had her first crush, I asked her what she liked about him and how it felt, and I shared her excitement by telling her it was normal and fun to experience those butterflies in her stomach. I told her about my first crush. When she was frustrated with a friend, I let her vent and prayed with her for discernment. I asked her if she wanted ideas about how to handle things with her friend. (This helped avoid unwanted advice and the eye roll.) Was I nervous that she was noticing boys? Of course! Was I angry that her friend was causing her hurt? Absolutely! But I didn't burden my daughter with my feelings. I took those things to my husband. He was *my* safe place to vent. I processed with him, prayed for my daughter, and talked with her as she wanted and needed.

When our children are nearing young adulthood, there are important things for them to learn. There are mistakes to be made that will lead to their own maturity. There are boundaries to be established as they assess how they want to live their lives. There is independence to be found as they separate themselves from their parents and find their own identities apart from us. As moms, we are wise to be patient and not steal these opportunities from our children as they navigate young adulthood. This is the journey of growing up—of learning, exploring, and experimenting—for them and us, and we must make sure we are their safe place to come back to when they fail or need encouragement and support.

INDIVIDUATION

Boundaries expert Dr. Henry Cloud explains the importance of individuation in his book *Boundaries*. He calls it an important and necessary process "as the child's need to see himself or herself as distinct from mother, a 'not me' experience ... You can't have a 'me' until you have a 'not-me'. For young adults to experience maturity and autonomy, they need to leave emotionally, spiritually, and physically. The individuation process requires something of the adult child and the parent. The adult child needs to leave to become mature and responsible, and the parent must release the child to become an independent person. It's this final stage of parenting that is the most difficult for many."[3]

We spend two decades knowing everything about our children but suddenly feel in the dark. This is a good sign that your child is on the road to healthy individuation. One friend said to me, "I used to know everything. He was my chatty one, and we would talk all the time. But suddenly he has become someone I don't recognize." Her twenty-three-year-old son was going to college across the country and was engaged to be married. It was a good thing he was changing. It was a sign that he was maturing and becoming a young man instead of the boy child she had known for the previous two decades. But it was hard for her. She was essentially saying she knew he was changing, but she didn't like it. I understand! She wanted him to be the same little boy he had always been. It was the shock that many parents feel when their children begin to distance themselves even though they themselves did the very same thing. But if we refuse to release our children to become adults, if we fail to empower them, it will have negative effects for both. The crux of the matter is this: Our children are figuring out who they are without us; we have to figure out who we are without them.

The "post-parental imperative" refers to the ongoing responsibilities and emotional connections parents feel after their children have grown up and left home, and it "demands that we make sense of who and what matters when we return to the self we put aside to raise our kids."[4] As parents who are negotiating new responsibilities while honoring the independence of their young adult children, this continuing sense of obligation may be both rewarding and difficult.

"Parenting skills were never designed to work for grown kids. We need to define the limits of our relationships with them and our involvement in their lives."[5] Here are some tips from *Doing Life with Your Adult Children* to help the process of individuation go more smoothly.[6]

- Strong criticism and judgmental statements paralyze growth.
- Change your role from parent-child to adult-adult.
- Cheer on their progress toward adult responsibility.

- Allow your adult children to control the amount of time they spend with you.
- Stop accommodating your children.
- Encourage hope.

This process of individuation takes us from dependence to independence. And remember, independence is the goal. It's a lifelong process toward wholeness. Viewing adulthood as a rite of passage will help our young adult children get there.

LETTING HIM BECOME A MAN

It goes without saying that sons are different than daughters. They need different things from their moms, and their relationships with us are different. Teenagers like to be treated as adults, and sons may need this sooner than daughters. We raise our sons to be men, so why do we try to stop that from happening as they become young adults by refusing to treat them as adults or simply acknowledging this stage of life?

What does it look like for a son to become a man? The Huffington Post addresses this question by discussing why sons seem to pull away from their mothers.

A son needs to emotionally separate from his mother (as does a mother from her son) so that he can grow into the man he needs to be. This often occurs on several levels and over a length of time. What this looks like and feels like to him is often very different from what it looks like and feels like to you, his mother.

He is not pulling away because he loves you less or wants you to feel excluded. Instead, as he matures and grows further into manhood, he feels the need and desire to share less. He is moving further into what being a man is for him and talking to his mother—sharing with her—is no longer something he wishes to do.

He loves you, but he is trying to figure out a different way to love you as a man, not as a boy. He can feel you making it harder for him to move forward (albeit unintentionally) and this just adds to his struggle. As a result, he may be short with you, irritated when you keep pressing, or even avoid your calls altogether.

He has transitioned into a man more than you realize. He sees himself as a "grown-up," and he wants you to see him that way, too—not as your child, but as your son who is a man. Setting boundaries, deciding where and how often he has contact with you, making decisions you are not happy with is not about you as much as it is about who he is as a man. It is his way of letting you know things are different now. His priorities are not your priorities.[7]

EMPOWERING HER AS A WOMAN

Mother/daughter relationships are the strongest among any parent/child relationship according to a study published in the Sage Journal. This is why their relationship serves as the cornerstone for the daughter's future relationships when she has learned healthy attachment and boundaries from her mother. Mothers teach their daughters how to trust their intuition, love themselves, care for others, and set healthy boundaries. And we do all of this as we empower them to make their own decisions and allow them to fail at times. It's through this process that our daughters learn to think for themselves, trust their intuition, and develop problem-solving skills. As our daughters leave their teenage years and become young adults, our role as moms transforms from advisor to consultant. It can be a fun season where we share more of our life experiences with our daughters as we help them navigate the young adult life. One young mom described the evolving relationship with her own mother this way:

As you get older, there comes a moment when you realize your mom is, in fact, imperfect. She battles the occasional insecurity. She says something she wishes she could take back and she has things she's processing inside—just like the rest of us.

It is in her imperfection that I have gotten to see her full humanity, and it is there that the container of our relationship has expanded. This is beautiful and hard. As a child, when I still saw my mom as infallible, things were constant and certain. Now, there is room for failure from both of us, and a new, more authentic and honest relationship has emerged.[8]

I have discovered the beauty of letting my daughter get to know me as a woman, not just as her mom, but I always keep in mind that I am her mom first. This means I do not burden her with my hurts and struggles, specifically as it relates to her growing up. I haven't always done it perfectly, but I continually strive to do it well. Perfection isn't the goal; progress is. She knows my heart struggles at times as she makes her own choices, but I don't overshare with her. In this season of my life, I am learning to think more about what I say and less about what I feel.

When my daughter graduated high school just a week after my grandma passed away, I had the opportunity to share with her how my relationship with my grandma had evolved during her seven months in at-home hospice. I told her how my grandma had become a safe place to share my momma heart and the struggle I was facing as my daughter prepared to leave home for college. "She would always say to me, 'You're gonna be okay,'" I told my daughter. "And I no longer have her voice to tell me that." My daughter was paying more attention than I realized because before she left for college, she gifted me with a bracelet that was inscribed with those very words: *You're gonna be okay.* It is one of my most treasured possessions. This story illustrates the beauty of an evolving adult-adult relationship with a young adult child.

There are times when I am cautious about how I react to my daughter's decisions. One time after college graduation, she scheduled three back-to-back trips, which meant she wouldn't be home for two weeks. It felt like a big deal because, at that point, she was engaged, and I heard the clock ticking down to how much time she had left at home. I wanted her to be home more than she was away, which she was, but it was a moment that hurt my heart. I took it as a sign that she didn't want to spend time with me, instead of realizing it had nothing to do with me and everything to do with her wanting to visit friends and her fiancé who all lived in different cities and/or states. We had an honest conversation about it, and ultimately, I took my hurting heart to the Lord (and to my husband) and allowed them to help me change my perspective so I could encourage her in her choices. It was yet another practice in letting go.

IT'S PAINFUL BUT NECESSARY

When we refuse to let go, we prevent our children from learning the skills they need to be successful in life; we hinder their growth into adulthood. Our primary job is to work ourselves out of a job—to prepare our children to be on their own—and if we don't, we have failed our responsibilities and our children. But knowing this doesn't make it any easier.

Author and mother Elizabeth Stone was right when she said, "Making the decision to have a child—it is momentous. It is to decide forever to have your heart go walking around outside your body."

This is how it should be. Children are supposed to grow up, separate from their parents, and be released into the world. Undoubtedly, there is the joy of watching them become their own unique individuals. Yet, there is a tearing away of the pieces of our hearts, which are forever knit to theirs. This is hard. It is one of those bittersweet rites of passage through which every mom must journey.

One blogger mom said it this way, "You see, all along I thought I was raising children, and it turns out I'm not. I am raising adults. I've been raising tiny humans to be good adults, and somehow that has changed my perspective on motherhood." And she's right—we don't raise sons to be sons; we don't raise daughters to be daughters—we raise our sons and daughters to be husbands and fathers, mothers and wives.

Stepping back is exactly what makes this stage of parenting so difficult. We aren't ready to let go, but they are ready to fly. That is the story of our lives as moms. Our children always seem to be more ready for the next stage than we are, and maybe that says something.

Let the closing words of this chapter—sentiments from other moms—simmer in your heart as you reflect on your experience of motherhood. These moms say it so well, capturing the angst and joy we feel as moms as we watch our children morph into young adults. As you read their honest words, I hope you embrace all of the emotions that come with watching your children become young adults. And give yourself permission to laugh and cry without apology.

> I didn't realize that I was teaching her how to get along without me. Then one day as she was getting the hang of riding her bike without training wheels and she asked me if she could ride ahead of me instead of beside me as I walked. I agreed without realizing that she could ride very well now. In a flash, she was gone down the street and I thought, "I'll only catch her now if she stops to wait for me." Which is exactly right. In a flash she's changed and will soon be gone and the only reason I catch up now is because she's waiting on me.
>
> ~ Tonya[9]

It feels like I won a ticket for the best seat in the house, but I was gone too long during intermission and missed part of the show. Or did I sleep through it? Or maybe I saw it all but just forgot a lot of the details.

It feels like both sorrow and joy.

It feels like a lump in my throat.

It feels like freedom, too.

And sometimes that part is hard for a mom to bear. Because now we have a little space to think, even though there's still a lot to do.

They are becoming themselves now and if we're paying attention, so are we. This is good and right. But can also feel confusing.

~ Emily[10]

When you witness your child making discoveries about themselves and the world, when you literally watch them becoming an adult before your eyes, your heart all but bursts with joy and gratitude.

But the truth is that a bursting heart feels an awful lot like a breaking one. The joy and the pain both pummel you harder than you expect them to. You think by now you should be used to this kind of emotional upheaval as your kids grow and change, but it never gets easier. There's nothing greater than watching your child walk toward their wide-open future, and nothing worse than watching them walk away from you.

~ Annie[11]

Being the mother of a son is like someone breaking up with you really slowly. Those aren't my words but they could be. I heard them in a movie recently called *The Otherhood* ... when I've spoken about this topic and repeated that quote, you can hear an instant, primal wave of audible gasps and yelps of pain coming from the audience. Those are the mothers of boys. Some of them still babies. Babies and toddlers and boys who will grow up and grow away and break up with their mothers. Slowly. But surely. Because they need to.

And if they do—when they do—it means we got it right. We parented them right. Whether you have sons or daughters, our role as parents is ultimately to make ourselves redundant.

But while we know they love us, their lives no longer spin around their mother as their main axis. We are not the sun around which they spin. Not anymore. It would be weird if we were. I know that. Logically.

~ Mia[12]

How's Your Heart?

1. Have you talked with your young adult child about expectations? Have you agreed on healthy boundaries?

2. How have you seen your son or daughter becoming separate (individuating) from you?

3. What would friendship with your young adult children look like to you?

4. Have you empowered your son and/or daughter to be the adult you raised them to be? How so?

Embrace Truth

Lord, Letting go of my young adult child is difficult, but I pray that by trusting you to be in control of his/her life, there will be peace in my heart. Please fill me with your fullness on days I feel empty. Help me trust that I'm letting go to a God who has always loved them and has always held them in his hands. I trust you not because of what I've done but because of who you are, Amen.

Do not exasperate your children; instead,
bring them up in the training and instruction of the Lord.
Ephesians 6:4

And let us consider how we may spur one another on toward
love and good deeds...
Hebrews 10:24

6

LESS IS SUCCESS

*Kids don't stay with you if you do it right. It's the one job where,
the better you are, the more surely you won't be needed in the long run.*
Barbara Kingsolver

I answered the phone late in the evening and heard crying on the other end. I knew it was my daughter calling, but I couldn't fathom what had caused her so much angst that she couldn't speak when I answered. She was attending college over an hour north of home and was just a few weeks into her freshman year. My girl rarely cries; she's always been a positive upbeat girl who sees the best of every situation. I knew it was serious when I heard her ragged sobs laced with fear. "Mom, I'm standing outside of my dorm building. I'm afraid to go inside." As she told me her life had been threatened by one of her roommates, a primal fear engulfed me and spurred me into action.

STEPPING IN

The best advice out there for parenting young adult children is this: Don't interfere. Allow them to think for themselves and make decisions and struggle and fail. It's through adversity that we learn best. And keep in mind, "There is a big difference between trying to fix your adult child's ongoing, self-created problems and helping a kid face a life crisis. An adult child who makes a poor decision—like a daughter who buys a Coach purse instead of paying her bills, or a son who gambles with his rent money—should learn from that decision. But then there are real family crises—auto accidents, illnesses, layoffs, house fires …"[1] when parents should get involved to support their young adult children. This doesn't mean we fix things for them; it means we are available for advice, guidance, or financial help. It means we allow them to need us less, and we accept it as part of our success.

If your young adult child is in danger, or about to make a dangerous, harmful, or irreversible decision, you should get involved. You don't want to take over and squash a learning experience, but making sure our young adult children are safe should be a priority.

That's what I did the evening I learned my daughter's life was being threatened and in the days that followed. I ensured her safety by talking with faculty and administrators, and I helped arrange a different living arrangement for her. All along the way, I asked her how or if she wanted me to get involved. Because she was eighteen, the college considered her an adult and was not inclined to involve me or her dad in the situation. It was with her permission that we navigated the difficult situation with her. But many situations followed that she would have to experience alone, including a university hearing to determine how the offending student would be held accountable.

LAND THE HELICOPTER

"Some of you need to land the helicopter," our pastor quipped one Sunday morning. I don't remember the context, but I remember the warning: Helicopter parenting can negatively impact a child's mental health, self-image, and coping skills.

> A new study from Florida State University found that kids who had helicopter parents were more likely to experience burnout from schoolwork, and they had a harder time transitioning from school to the real world. The irony is, when kids are micro-managed by their parents, they don't develop 'self-control skills' that are necessary for reaching long-term goals and coping with academic stressors … Other studies have shown that young adults (in their college years) who have helicopter parents have lower levels of self-efficacy, which is the personal belief that they're capable of handling tough life tasks and decisions. They also experience more anxiety and depression, and lower levels of life satisfaction and physical health.[2]

The term *helicopter parent* was used as early as 1969[3] but gained popularity in 1990 with the book *Parenting with Love and Logic*. It became known as the parenting style of the baby boomer generation, which means millennials were the first generation to be helicopter-parented.[4] Helicopter parents give their children everything growing up except for the ability to think and cope on their own. They are given everything except a sense of self, which is exactly what the following article describes.

> How could helicopter parents, in their loving myopic vision, know that they were handicapping their children with years of constant micro-management? They tried to make their future lawyer or artist stand out from the

other Sophies, even if that meant costly college advisors, therapists, IEP lawsuits, fraud, lies … kids were always busy, busy, busy with after-school activities, there was little room for spontaneous interactions in which a child would call upon their own resources to respond appropriately. They were always being watched. Adults told them to play nice, so they did. Such nice kids. Unsupervised play was unheard of and never given the gravitas it has in healthy childhood development. These children would be given every advantage and would never be in danger. Kids weren't allowed to go anywhere on their own, and in many places, there is nowhere to 'explore.' [My generation] learned to navigate the world, avoid weirdos, observe nature, get dirty, ask questions, and socialize without parental interference … The overprotectiveness that allowed parents to 'manage' their kids turned out to not be in their best interests.[5]

When we over-protect our children, they fail to learn how to take care of themselves; when we do too much for them, they fail to learn how to do things for themselves. This leads to them growing up with a lack of confidence and growing anxiety around minimal challenges. If we truly want the best for our children, we must focus on making them more resilient and empowered.

A friend of mine shared about the first time she left her daughter home alone. She was going next door to visit with a sick neighbor, but her daughter told her she was very uncomfortable with the situation. She began to melt down at the thought of being in the house alone. She was sixteen years old.

One of my daughter's college friends shared how her parents insisted she have *Life 360* on her phone—an app that tracks more than just your whereabouts. She said it was not uncommon for her mom to call when she was driving and say, "You're driving too fast." Or she would be at Target and her mom would call and ask what she was buying. The girl was a twenty-year-old college student.

And one dad who was a policeman shared this story: "I was working graduation at the Air Force Academy, and part of my job was to protect the cadets. We kept a safety buffer between where they gathered and the general public. I had a mom insist she needed to get to her son. When I asked what the urgency was, she pulled out a bottle of sunscreen and said, 'I have to get this to him or he's going to get sunburned.' I assured her that if he was about to be commissioned as an officer in the United States Air Force, he would know how to take care of himself. And if he didn't, he better learn quickly."

BUT I NEED DIRECTION

Maybe you can relate and think those parents are doing all the right things. Or maybe you cringe because you see it as over-reaching parenting. Some of you wonder if there is such a thing. I recently read *The Book of Charlie* and in talking about the way Charlie's single mom raised him compared to the author's upbringing, he said, "By today's standards, though, she would seem almost neglectful. In Charlie's memory, her parenting boiled down to a single all-purpose piece of advice: 'Just do the right thing.' This simplicity is so removed from my own generation of helicopter parents. My parenting mistakes … stem from overinvolvement rather than benign neglect."[6]

Benign Neglect. How many generations before our children's grew up that way? Where we rode bikes all over the neighborhood after school and knew to be home in time for dinner. Where our parents went to school all day and then straight to their after-school jobs to help pay the bills. Where our grandparents didn't make it through high school because they had to help run the family farm? *Overinvolvement* is not a term that prior generations would be familiar with.

Dr. Jane Adams, who would be the same generation as my parents, said this about raising her children: "Mindful of the ambitions our parents had for us, and the sometimes heavy-handed way they tried to persuade us in what they thought were the right directions, we resolved to let our children make up their own minds about their future."[7]

I wonder if that explains a little of my upbringing. I didn't have helicopter parents; it often felt the opposite—although I would not have been able to articulate it that way as a teenager—but I remember times of wishing my parents would give me more direction. They were supportive and loving and prayed for me, and they empowered me to make my own choices. I don't know if that was intentional or just a function of a family where Dad traveled a lot and Mom was caring for four kids while also being involved in everything we did—from PTA president to youth leader at church to chauffer for all of us kids and our friends. Or maybe I'm to blame, and they chose that path of parenting for me specifically. After all, when I was five years old and my mom took me to my first day of kindergarten, I told her not to walk me to the door. I wasn't embarrassed by her; I was exercising my independence. As a mom, I say, "Well done, Mom and Dad, for letting me do so." I had an independent mom who taught me the same and a dad who instilled a high value on education and making my own choices.

WHAT'S GOING ON?

A recent study found that 54% of eighteen- to twenty-five-year-olds are still living with their parents.[8] And *failure to launch* is a new term that describes the inability of millions of young people—even those with jobs—to fully transition into independent adults.[9] (Yes, the movie *Failure to Launch* comes to mind.) One recent study suggested one in five, or 20% of college graduates, took a parent with them to a job interview.[10] What? What are we doing as parents? My first instinct was to yell, "Stop it!" Not to the young adults but to the parents! Does this say more about the parents than their children? Are we more concerned with their happiness than their success?

Parents have no rightful place at job interviews with their young adult children. If they ask you to go, it is your job to say no.

We have to let our children feel discomfort and struggle, allowing them to be disappointed, and helping them work through failure. And we have to let them do the tasks they are capable of—making their beds, doing their laundry, and packing their lunches. As parents, we have to say no. Say no to joining them on a job interview. Or calling college professors about grades. Or cleaning their rooms. It's time to allow our young adult children to be young adults. And when they come to us with a problem, learn to say these four empowering words: *I believe in you!* Every young adult needs to be validated as they are learning to navigate the adult world. Maybe more so. Saying, "I believe in you," is a great way to encourage, validate, and support your young adult child in making decisions. Validation increases self-esteem, improves trust, resilience, and motivation, and helps with mental health.

One friend told me she regularly said, "I believe in you," to her son after college graduation, and she took it a step further by saying, "I believe in your choices." She wanted him to feel confident that he could make good choices and pivot if they turned out not so good.

The traumatic evening that my daughter's freshman year was turned upside down spiraled into an arduous ordeal that would affect our entire family for many months. There were multiple moves—on and off campus—restraining orders, hearings, and countless meetings, phone calls, and email communications with numerous faculty and administrators. I prayed for my daughter's fearful, broken heart. I sought the Lord daily, and I begged him to intervene. I was literally on my face in prayer every single day.

Surrender had become such a large part of my daily life that I often held my hands palm up in a physical gesture of letting go. I knew I had to let God have full control of her situation. I went to bat for her many times after the threat happened, but I felt completely powerless. I told her, "I'm so sorry I can't fix this for you. But I think that's the point. God wants you to trust *him* with the outcome." And therein lies the deepest truth and hardest surrender, God has lessons for our young adult children that they can only learn through trials.

One of the best things we can do for our young adult children is promote their own self-empowerment and independence by encouraging them to take an active role in addressing challenges and finding solutions. As moms, we can help them identify their strengths and let them know we believe they are capable of handling whatever it is they face. It's important to know the difference between helping and enabling.[11]

If the situation isn't life-threatening or dangerous, these tips from *Psychology Today* can help you engage with your young adult child without enabling them.[12]

1. Listen without trying to fix things immediately.
2. Offer support without conditions.
3. Encourage their efforts, no matter how small.
4. Respect their journey and autonomy.
5. Provide practical help when appropriate.
6. Share your own experiences and vulnerabilities.
7. Encourage professional support when necessary.
8. Stay connected through shared interests.
9. Set healthy boundaries for your relationship.
10. Remain patient and avoid pushing for change.

We have to accept this truth: "We cannot make our grown kids happy. As long as we expect that we can, they will, too. And we will both be disappointed."[13] Surrendering our young adult children into the hands of the One who is writing their stories is the best choice we can make as moms. Reminding ourselves over and over of his trustworthiness and good plans goes a long way to help us navigate the journey of surrender.

How's Your Heart?

1. Have you experienced a time with your young adult child when you needed to step in and help navigate a difficult situation? How did your child respond?

2. Were your parents helicopter parents? Do you consider yourself a helicopter mom?

3. What would it look like for you to "land the helicopter" and empower your young adult children to make their own choices?

4. How do you feel about the term *overinvolvement* when it comes to parenting?

Embrace Truth

Lord, I don't really know how to let go. I want to give you control of my life and my children, but I'm struggling. I come to you with a humble heart to admit that I can do nothing in my own strength. Teach me how to submit my life to you. Show me how to abide in you day by day, and instruct me how to live in spirit and truth. Help me give control of my life and my children to you in every way. I pray that your truth will guide me in this season of life, Amen.

For the Spirit God gave us does not make us timid,
but gives us power, love and self-discipline.
2 Timothy 1:7

Humble yourselves before the Lord and he will lift you up.
James 4:10

7

HOW HEALTHY ARE WE?

People are just as happy as they make up their minds to be.
Abraham Lincoln

As our children move into young adulthood, they need us less and less. And for a mom who found her purpose and identity in being a mom, this can feel devastating. Dare I say we might even feel betrayed by our children when they do the very things we raised them to do? When our young adult children begin to live in the adult world, whether going to college, moving out on their own, or starting a full-time job while living at home, they will need us less. And this creates a void of time and energy. It's up to us as moms to figure out the next steps. Just as we are not responsible for our children's happiness, they are not responsible for ours.

BEAUTIFUL BUT CHALLENGING

Every single person needs love, connection, and significance. As a mom raising children, these needs were filled by them needing you. Those needs don't go away when they grow up and leave home, but we have to find new healthy ways to have our needs met as moms. It's not up to our children to make us feel fulfilled.

Without even realizing it, we can begin to relate to our young adult children with passive-aggressive behavior and comments, act rejected, and play the martyr. But at best, it will backfire and alienate us from our growing and maturing young adult children. At worst, it will teach them unhealthy ways of interacting with others. We can't expect to raise emotionally healthy children if we are not emotionally healthy first.

As Dr. Laurence Steinberg says, we are in our children's psyche. We know when the guilt card will work, how to manipulate their behavior with strings-attached gifts, or that calling names will break their insubordination. It's all a very immature and unhealthy way to parent. But what's the alternative? We have to find healthy alternatives to repressing, denying, and acting hurt and rejected.

Honest communication about how you are feeling will go a long way with your young adult children. Ask them for understanding and patience as you learn to let go. This isn't to burden your children with your feelings; they are not responsible for how you are feeling. This is to acknowledge to them that you are aware of the struggle and are working to get through it in a healthy way.

Ask yourself, "Is my child happy and thriving?" If the answer is yes, it will take the focus off your own feelings and shift to being happy for your child and the new life he/she is building. Being a mom is a constant exercise in selflessness. We continuously lay aside our needs to take care of those of our children. Their leaving home is no different. Them leaving home is the culmination of the hard work you have done over the past eighteen-plus years. Focusing on your young adult child's success and growth will help your heart smile rather than break.

Gratitude is another great way to shift your focus, which also has healing effects by changing the neural structure of the brain. Neuroscience has made the connection between gratitude and the "feel good" chemicals in our brains—dopamine and serotonin—which is almost as effective as medication. What does that even mean? Simply put, gratitude decreases stress, improves quality sleep, releases toxic emotions, and reduces pain, anxiety, and depression.[1] Keeping a gratitude journal might be an important key to emotional health in this season of life.

When we as moms are not happy and fulfilled, we can create unhealthy attachments to our children and look to them to meet our desire for attention, affection, companionship, and control. So, when they leave home and begin to forge a new life and new relationships, we perceive a threat to our desires being met. We cannot depend on our children for our happiness.

It's a beautiful but challenging phase of life. And we have to be mindful to avoid destructive behaviors. For example, many moms focus on the past and get stuck in their grief over what they perceive they are losing. It's easy to become nostalgic about raising our children and wishing they were still little and dependent on us. After all, it gave us purpose to feel so needed. But this can hinder us from being present in the moment and the new phase of parenting we are entering. Our children still need us, but it looks different. They need us to bounce ideas off of, to be their cheerleader as they try new things, and to encourage them when they are down or fearful. We can feel we are losing our children as they become young adults.

Instead, focus on what you have—a new evolving relationship. Even if it's not what you had hoped it would be, what is something you can be grateful for concerning your young adult child? Is he making new friends? Did she start a new job? Do you see her making good decisions with her money? Does he make an effort to text or call occasionally? We can always find things to be grateful for when we look for them.

THE WILDERNESS

Transitioning through the stages of parenting—from the teen years to college to an empty nest—can feel like a wilderness. And let's face it, no one enjoys the wilderness. But it's in those barren places of the soul that we can heal and learn to thrive. "The wilderness where faith can thrive is the very desert where it can dry up and die if we are not watchful."[2] It's up to us to choose the orientation of our hearts—growth or decline, surrender or obstinance toward the One who is making a way through the desert.[3] The following quote sheds light on the purpose of wilderness times.

> The wilderness exposes what's inside these chests of ours like little else does. It is frighteningly easy to give lip service to God while our hearts are lost in his gifts [our children]...while the tendrils of our heart slowly wrap themselves around a marriage, a friend-ship, or a career [again, our children]—scarcely recog-nizable, almost incurable. Psalm 25: 10 instructs us, "All the paths of the Lord are steadfast love and faithful-ness." *All the paths*—even the ones that take us through the desert. Steadfast love has brought you here, and he will never leave you nor forsake you.[4]

This season of life may not be a wilderness for you. Perhaps you are sailing through it with relative ease. Or maybe you are grieving but have confidence in your next steps, your next season of life. But if you are feeling lost and uncertain—like you're in a wilderness—take heart. Good things come out of these barren places.

The wilderness is a place of preparation. During these times, God often withholds or removes that which we have come to depend on other than him. Without realizing it, that can often be our children or our role as their mothers. God wants us to turn to him and seek his purpose and will for our lives, just as he wants our young adult children to do the same. The wilderness is also a place of revelation. It's in these barren places when we are desperate for more of him that he reveals his will for us. When we are lost, he gives direction. When we are hopeless, he gives hope. When we are empty, he fills us. If you are longing to know your purpose, you are in the perfect place to hear from the Lord. He promises to answer when we call on him.[5] It is in the wilderness that God speaks tenderly to our hearts. Lastly, the wilderness is a place of surrender. It is a place where we learn to trust and put ourselves and our children fully in his hands. Will you open your hands and receive what God has for you? As C.S. Lewis once said, "You have to let go at some point in order to move forward."

EMOTIONAL HEALTH MATTERS

Our children need to have a sense of control and choice in their lives. We need to allow them to undergo "safe suffering." By the time they leave home, they should feel a deep sense of personal responsibility for their lives. So, don't negate that by taking back control of their choices. Let them choose what classes to take in college, what job to accept, how to spend their money, what friends to spend time with, and where to spend weekends or time off from school.

Be an emotionally healthy mom by choosing emotionally healthy behaviors. Even when you get it wrong, you can always start again (and apologize when necessary). Here are some positive traits of emotionally healthy mothers to consider:

- Listens more than she talks.
  She asks questions to clarify, which helps her child
  process what they are going through. Asking open-
  ended questions is a great way to learn more about
  what they are thinking and feeling. And this is a
  great time to practice active listening skills —

paraphrasing and reflecting back what you have
heard.

- Encourages instead of criticizes.
  It's easy to think our young adult children are doing
  it wrong when they do something differently than
  we would. But instead of saying that, we can
  encourage them with words like, "I believe in you,"
  "I'm proud of you for trying," or "That must be
  really hard, but I believe you can handle it."

- Doesn't offer unsolicited advice.
  As moms, we have opinions about almost everything
  involving our children. And we have experience.
  But just as we learned so much about life through
  our experiences, we must allow our young adult
  children to do the same. Don't rob your young adult
  children of growth opportunities because it is hard
  for you to see them struggle.

- Doesn't burden her children with her emotions.
  It's not our young adult child's responsibility to fix
  how we feel, carry our pain, or help us through the
  struggle of changing seasons. They have their own
  warring emotions about adulthood and their new
  season of life. Make space for them to share what
  they are feeling. It's okay to be honest about how
  we are feeling, but don't make it their burden to
  carry.

When it comes to advice and wanting to guide our young adult
children, it matters what we say and how we say it. Instead of
saying, "This is what you should do," try asking, "Would you
like to hear my thoughts?" This empowers our young adult
children to invite us to share. If they don't, we are wise to not

share our thoughts. But we can take comfort in knowing we have conveyed to our young adult children that we are there for guidance if/when they do ask for it. Many moms take the view that they no longer play an important role in their young adult child's life because they are no longer calling the shots. That's not the case. Our role has shifted to that of a trusted advisor.

They need to know we believe they can handle difficult situations. David Narang, a clinical psychologist in West L.A. says the key to building a strong relationship with adult children is to think of yourself as "a sounding board for a powerful adult" rather than "a rescuer for a helpless child." They need to feel they have been heard before we can offer any type of guidance. They want our support, such as, "I bet you are frustrated with that. I would be too." We should operate under the assumption that our young adult children can handle the situations they are facing. In fact, if we have done our job well of raising competent, empowered children, they will be able to handle difficult situations with little input from us—their moms. It's an opportunity to let our young adult children put into practice what we have taught and modeled. We must be careful to not steal opportunities for growth from them. We should be a safe place for them to talk about their struggles, and then we can help them arrive at their own solutions. As moms, we have a unique position to help our children feel supported and capable with their own inner strength.

We should never attempt to make our young adult children feel responsible for our parenting mistakes or emotions. Validating their perspective doesn't mean we agree with them. It means we hear them and recognize they have a right to feel how they feel. And don't we all want to feel heard? Parenting young adult children is an opportunity to choose healthy behaviors and give up the unhealthy ones that negatively impact everyone involved. "Healthy habits are learned in the same way as unhealthy ones—through practice."[6] Let's practice being emotionally healthy moms!

How's Your Heart?

1. On a scale of 1-5, how emotionally healthy are you?

2. Does this season of life feel like a wilderness? If not, what does it feel like? What is God revealing to you in this season of life?

3. What healthy behaviors or things to avoid are difficult for you? How can you practice embracing healthy behaviors and giving up negative ones?

4. What can you be grateful for in this season of life? Consider starting a gratitude journal to help you focus on the positives and remain open to new things.

Embrace Truth

Lord, I don't want to overlook the paths you carve out in the wilderness. Give me a glimpse of the Holy Spirit moving. During this season, open my eyes to your vision of a happy and prosperous future for me and my children. Thank you for doing something new in my life. I am grateful for your presence. While I travel this path to a new normal, fill my soul with joy, Amen.

You, God, are my God,
earnestly I seek you;
I thirst for you,
my whole being longs for you,
in a dry and parched land
where there is no water.
Psalm 63:1

See, I am doing a new thing!
Now it springs up; do you not perceive it?
I am making a way in the wilderness
and streams in the wasteland.
Isaiah 43:19

8

MADE FOR A PURPOSE

*The two most important days in life are the day you were born
and the day you find out why.*
Mark Twain

W hat comes to mind when you hear the word *purpose*? Do you immediately think of motherhood? Or your career? Or your friends and family? Do you think of books like *The Purpose Driven Life*? Or do you struggle to know your purpose?

Let me tell you this: Your kids are not your purpose. I know, some of you just gasped and nearly abandoned this book. But let me say it again: No other person is your purpose, even your children. Once you have children, motherhood is for a lifetime; raising them is for a season—a temporary assignment—one that we pour our hearts into. No other relationship in life is as all-consuming as motherhood.

Motherhood is a responsibility. It is a role to be taken seriously, but it is not your purpose. Your purpose is not defined by any role in your life. Your purpose is never limited by the roles you fill. It's bigger than what you do. It is "meaningful enough to take you through the changing seasons of life. Your purpose is meaningful enough to give you a reason to be excited even in the hardest seasons."[1] Your purpose is found in who you are. It's the impact you make on others. This is a season of life where we have to—*get to*—focus on what's next. Not for our children; for ourselves.

Your purpose is knit into your DNA by the Creator. "You didn't create yourself, so there is no way you can tell yourself what you were created for! If I handed you an invention you had never seen before, you wouldn't know its purpose, and the invention itself wouldn't be able to tell you either. Only the creator or the owner's manual could reveal its purpose," wrote Rick Warren, author of *The Purpose Drive Life*. He added, "The easiest way to discover the purpose of an invention is to ask the creator of it. The same is true for discovering your life's purpose: Ask God." If you want to know your true purpose, you have to turn to the One who created you for a purpose.

FINDING MEANING

When we put our purpose on our children's shoulders, we place a burden on them they were never meant to carry—a burden they *can't* carry. Our children were created with their own purpose, and we have to be careful as moms that we don't hinder them from finding it by making them ours. Think about it: If teaching others in our jobs is our purpose, when we leave that job, we leave our purpose. If serving others through volunteering is our purpose, when we stop volunteering, we stop having purpose. If raising our children is our purpose, when they grow up and leave home, we lose our purpose. This is not how it's supposed to be.

One mother of seven—LJ—understood this well from her experience of having a mom who did just that. She decided, "I will not saddle [my children] with the burden of giving me meaning in my life. I will not burden them with being my universe, my world. The responsibility for my happiness and sense of purpose is on me, not my children. It would not be fair to them to have that weight. I want them to see me living with purpose and meaning that isn't dependent on them—includes them, yes, but not dependent on them."[2]

LJ came to this conclusion after seeing how her mother had made her children her whole world, her sole purpose in life, and the effects it had on her later in life. She said, "When my siblings and I left home, it nearly destroyed my mother. It took years for her to really find something she was passionate about that inspired her. It was a caregiving role again; she raises and trains guide dog puppies and she's really good at it. Those dogs are her world." Ah, there it is—purpose! LJ's mom had it all along, she just didn't understand it, and she let it hinge on her children instead of its true source—caring for others.

I want to tell you about an ambitious, driven, and successful lawyer who went from prosecuting Fortune 500 executives to being a stay-at-home mom and how she realized where her purpose lay. She was surprised to find motherhood came easily to her. She couldn't relate to the moms who talked about how difficult raising children was. "Nothing had ever felt so natural, like I was doing exactly what I was always meant to do," she wrote in a Huffington Post article. "My all-encompassing idea of professional success morphed from prestige and money to freedom and flexibility, and I just loved how being a parent blunted my need to accomplish and succeed profession-ally." Then she said this, the realization we all must come to as moms, "The problem with kids, however, is if you feed and water them, eventually they grow up and out."

She shared how she didn't expect it to come so fast and how she felt "smacked in the face" by her children growing up and needing her less. So, she went on a journey to find her purpose by identifying her core values. What she found was a profound realization that maybe you can relate to. "I realized … my purpose had always been about human potential and connection. In raising my kids, I was 100% aligned with my core values, and without realizing it, I'd been living my purpose the entire time."[3]

Psychologists agree, "The primary purpose of parenting is to raise fully functional adults who can take care of themselves and make a positive contribution to society."[4] While we are raising our children, it is our most important role. And we can tap into our purpose while we are doing it. We can live out our purpose even while raising our children. We can be passionate about raising our children (it will help us do it well), and we can look at it as our most important job in that season of life, but we must be careful to not confuse being a mother with our purpose. Our purpose is an integral part of who we are; it's not what we do.

A WAY OF LIFE

As I mentioned earlier, we have to turn to God and ask him what our purpose is if we are struggling to know what it is. We have to dive into his Word to know what he says about purpose. As God's created people, we have a common purpose —to act justly, love mercy, and walk humbly with God.[5] We also were created to rule over creation and produce godly offspring.[6] Isaiah 43:7 tells us we were created for God's glory. Solomon, considered the wisest man who ever lived, said, "The whole duty of man is to fear God and his commandments."[7] And Ephesians 2:10 says, "We are God's workmanship, created in Christ Jesus to do good works, which he prepared in advance as our way of life." We were created to do good; our purpose is a way of life; it's a heart posture, not a career path. So, what does that look like when we are trying to launch our children into young adulthood? What does it look like when they leave home?

Consider this: "If you're feeling purposeless ... chances are you haven't had the opportunity to impact others in a way that is natural to you."[8] I love that—in a way that is *natural* to you! When we know our purpose and live in our purpose, it won't feel like work. It won't be something we have to do; it's something we get to do—something we look forward to.

When my younger brother was starting his career as a pastor, I often listened to his sermons and always thought he was a gifted communicator and a talented creator of stories. He was following God's calling for his life. But it wasn't until he went through a painful season of changing churches that I heard him preach and thought, "This is what it looks like to live *in* your calling." His purpose wasn't just something he followed; it became how he lived.

As a chiropractor, my husband is fulfilling his calling by caring for hurting, sick people. (Not surprisingly, his office motto is, "Serving God by caring for his people.") But he will tell you that his purpose is to give people hope through quality healthcare. He goes to work each day, but it never feels like work. He likes to say he is an ordained chiropractor—it's what he was made to do. His purpose isn't the profession; it's how God works through him to serve others and use his gifts.

In the year leading up to my daughter leaving for college and my son completing his last year of homeschooling, I knew I would have time on my hands that I needed to fill so I wouldn't feel lost. So, I began to pray for direction and asked the Lord to open doors for a part-time job I could do from home. I wasn't even looking for purpose; I was looking for a distraction and thought it would be great to make a little money. Within months, I received an opportunity for a grant writing job—something I had done years prior to having children. I said yes to that job, which wasn't particularly fulfilling, but it gave me something to do for a good cause. Within that first year of being back to work as a stay-at-home mom, I began to pray for an opportunity that would be more fulfilling —an opportunity to live in my purpose—and God answered by reconnecting me with an old friend and introducing me to a new friend, all of which led to my dream job as a book editor. It's the type of work that makes me excited to get out of bed every morning. It's something I am good at and satisfies that deep longing to use my gifts and talents to serve others. That's purpose!

If you feel like you don't know your purpose or how to discover it, ponder the following questions.[9]

1. What is the most rewarding thing you've ever done for someone else? Why was it rewarding?
    - Did you cook meals all week for a friend who was recovering from surgery?
    - Did you help your grandparents record their memories in a journal or scrapbook?
    - Did you stay up all night talking to a friend who was going through a difficult time, reminding them that they aren't alone?

2. How do others describe your impact on their lives?
    - What things have people specifically asked you for?
    - How do people describe you?
    - When have you improved someone's mood?

3. If you had all the time in the world to volunteer, who would you volunteer for?
    - What kind of impact do you want to make on the world?
    - Who are you passionate about serving? Orphans? Elderly? Homeless?

4. What moments in your life have been the hardest? Why?
    - Our hardships often become our causes because we don't want others to experience the same pain we did. Were you bullied as a child? Did your mom die of cancer? Were you homeless after losing your house in a fire?

- The hardest things we face are often the things we want to change in the world.

Remember, your "purpose is how you know you're changing the world: because you're changing lives, one human at a time."[10] And the easiest way to know your purpose is to ask the One who made you. Follow the New Testament instruction for seeking answers: "Keep on asking, and you will receive what you ask for. Keep on seeking, and you will find. Keep on knocking, and the door will be opened to you. For everyone who asks, receives. Everyone who seeks, finds. And to everyone who knocks, the door will be opened."[11]

How's Your Heart?

1. Do you know your purpose? What helped you know what it is?

2. Have you talked with your young adult children about their purpose?

3. What steps could you take today to embrace your purpose?

4. Are you ready and/or willing to embrace a new purpose for the next season of life?

Embrace Truth

Lord, As I begin to take steps toward my purpose, I ask for your wisdom in every small and large decision. Reveal my true purpose in your perfect timing. I ask for your guidance and thank you for the gift and power of the Holy Spirit. Thank you that I don't have to rely on my own understanding, as your wisdom will guide me each step of the way, Amen.

The LORD himself goes before you and will be with you; he will never leave you nor forsake you. Do not be afraid; do not be discouraged.
Deuteronomy 31:8

"For I know the plans I have for you," declares the LORD, "plans to prosper you and not to harm you, plans to give you hope and a future."
Jeremiah 29:11

9

LOVING A PRODIGAL

It's the Holy Spirit's job to convict,
God's job to judge, and my job to love.
Billy Graham

We all have times as our children grow and begin to make their own decisions when we cringe at their choices. Even "good" children make poor choices sometimes. They may do or say things we wished they wouldn't, and they may make choices that contradict the values we tried to instill in them as children. "They [operate] on emotion and impulse as they [push] toward adulthood with bodies ready for the challenge but brains lagging far behind."[1] And what of the child who walks away from their faith or denies God entirely? What if they cut off all communication because they feel judged?

I recently listened to a podcast where a father and son discussed their vast theological differences. They were living with opposing morals and easily could have severed their relationship in the pursuit of being right. But the father was intent on loving his son like Jesus, and the son was determined to maintain a civil relationship with his parents. He spoke of the current culture that celebrates cutting off your parents and described it as "an act of profound self-harm" because it doesn't resolve the pain; it exports it to other people and cuts off the potential for healing. When you cut yourself off from people who disagree with you, you cut yourself off from your greatest teachers—people who can teach you to love, be compassionate and patient, and ask good questions. Navigating differences in a relationship is a great time to follow Stephen Covey's advice to seek to understand before seeking to be understood. The father explained his mindset by saying, "We don't say we agree to disagree. We say, 'We agree *that* we disagree.'"

So, how do we respond to the prodigal child? I haven't walked the road of a parent with a prodigal child, but I have been that child. As we are all prone to do at various times in our lives, I sought to have control of my life and turned my back on the values I was raised with. I have refused the Holy Spirit in my life; I have run from the truth. Our hearts are prone to wander, and without the Lord's saving grace, we are destined to eternal separation from him. But God.

It is not my intention to offer trite advice for parents of prodigal children. What I do offer is the wisdom of the ages that we can apply to our relationships with our young adult children despite the circumstances. We are not their Holy Spirit; there is one Holy Spirit, and he alone brings conviction to the hearts of his children. He is pursuing our children even when we don't perceive it. And he is writing their story—a different story from our own. So, we have to be careful to not try to make our children into our image, wanting them to do things like we did or according to our will. Each one of us is uniquely made in the image of God, and he has a unique calling on each of our lives. We are called to be like Jesus, and Jesus is love!

That being said, tremendous heartache often follows when our young adult children don't take the same path as us or they make decisions we don't want them to make. I'd encourage you to keep in mind that maintaining a relationship is paramount. As long as your children are still talking to you, even if it's not harmonious, you still have a voice. We have to be cautious to not use that voice to condemn or shame but to champion and encourage our young adult children. To bless them even when we don't feel they are deserving; to affirm the gifts in their lives, even when it doesn't seem they are using them for good. As the Bible counsels, anger does not produce righteousness.[2] Grace is never a poor choice.

FINDING HOPE

The following is a portion of a profound liturgy for parents who are living with a prodigal child or navigating a strained relationship. Let these words be the instruction and encouragement you need if you are walking a difficult path with your young adult children.

> Lord … I feel a rift in such fellowship
> with one I have long held dear.
> As our beliefs have unexpectedly diverged.
> what once seemed foundational and permanent
> in our bond is shaken and cracked;
> gone is the comfort and ease we once shared.
> Now I bear this growing ache of separation,
> since what matters so much to me conflicts
> with what matters so much to my loved one.
> I am lost and confused.
> I do not understand how they could reject
> what seems so good to me, so evident.
>
> Though it may grate against my pride,
> make me willing to consider where I might
> … have wrongly assumed I understood
> another's heart, or where I have dismissed

their position too easily… Let me listen well,
speak from compassion rather than fear or
defensiveness, and quickly confess where I have
failed to love as you have called me to do.

Lord, help me seek to understand
more than I seek to be understood.
Remind me that this person I have loved
so long is not now my enemy.
Whether they are right or wrong in their beliefs,
my path is to pray, not to condemn.

… You love this person more than I ever could,
and so I give them back to you.

Their story is not mine.
You alone know their journey's turns;
you alone can save and guide.
You have created them with such care and
delight, and I recall times of delight we once
shared, remembering how your image shone so
clearly in my loved one's face.

Let me not attempt to force them now
into my own image, but teach me to trust
that you keep reaching out to them
even when I discern no immediate
evidence of your movements.[3]

ANCHORED IN LOVE

Loving a prodigal child at any age is a journey of resilience,
hope, and unconditional love. It's something we can do only
through the power of the Holy Spirit because it is difficult—
even counterintuitive—to love people who cause us strife.
Although we can't control our young adult children's choices,

we can control how we respond and support them through their journey. Demonstrating unwavering love for our young adult children as they make their own choices can act as a powerful anchor, even in the face of poor decisions. And don't we all need to be anchored to someone who loves us? Especially when we are adrift (and maybe don't realize it)? You are free to love your young adult children without an agenda.

I've heard countless stories from parents and young adults who are all struggling with the tension of unmet expectations, feelings of loss and rejection, and the desire to be understood and heard.

- The daughter who moved across the country and cut off communication because she felt harshly judged and rejected by her parents.
- The son who decided he wanted to live as a woman and cut off his family in the process.
- The son who would rather struggle to make ends meet over the summer instead of going home during college break because his parents criticized his every move.
- The daughter who married her boyfriend two months after they met and didn't tell her parents until it was all said and done.

These are all difficult situations to navigate and should be done with the support of trusted counselors, pastors, and friends. But there is hope. Perhaps it starts with forgiveness.

"Forgiving our kids their trespasses against our values, our hopes, our assumptions, and expectations is a gift we give ourselves, not them. Forgiveness allows us to let go and move on after grieving not only the loss of our dreams for them but also those we had for ourselves. And that is a task that falls to us in this season of our life regardless of whether our grown kids are exactly who we always hoped they would be or not."[4]

Every one of us wants to feel valued and understood. So,

love your young adult child for who they are, not for their actions. As you navigate this journey, have patience with both yourself and your young adult child. Constant reminders or criticisms can push them further away. Offer support and encouragement, and let them know they always have a seat at the table within their family (for this is the same heart Jesus has toward each one of us—and our own hearts are prone to wander). We can love our young adult children just as Christ loves us—not because we are worthy but because he is gracious and merciful.

What better way to point them to the Savior than to love them unconditionally? And I get it, loving conditionally is emotionally easier than letting go of our conditions. But the potential for harm is always lurking; that's not how Jesus taught us to love. May we "find the grace to hold on to our own convictions and have enough grace to let [our young adult children] do the same."[5]

How's Your Heart?

1. Does the theme of release and surrender in the above liturgy fill you with hope and comfort or fear and uncertainty? Can you choose to surrender your prodigal child into God's hands and rest in the shadow of the Almighty?

2. How has the Holy Spirit led you through this difficult season?

3. Can you view this difficult path as an invitation to grow in faith and grace?

4. Can you choose to love your prodigal child with grace despite their choices?

Embrace Truth

Lord, I want to love my child well, but I need you to fill me with grace and forgiveness. Shape my deeply rooted beliefs by your truth, and help me extend the same grace that has been given to me. Remind me to carry my frustrations and disappointments to you rather than lashing out at my beloved. I trust you to protect my child as you woo him/her with your abundant love, Amen.

Whoever dwells in the shelter of the Most High
will rest in the shadow of the Almighty.
I will say of the LORD, "He is my refuge and my fortress,
my God, in whom I trust."
Psalm 91:1-2

"For my thoughts are not your thoughts,
neither are your ways my ways,"
declares the LORD.
"As the heavens are higher than the earth,
so are my ways higher than your ways
and my thoughts than your thoughts."
Isaiah 55:8-9

There's a song by NEEDTOBREATHE called "Banks," and it is a profound metaphor that describes life as a river. The lyrics paint the picture of a river that is sometimes calm and others turbulent, but there is a desire to be like the banks of a river—"I wanna hold you close, but never hold you back, just like the banks to the river."

A few of the members of the band wrote the song for their wives essentially saying, "When the current gets strong, I will be there; when the current is gentle, I will be there." One of the band members and authors of the song, Bear Rinehart, explained to *American Songwriter*, "It is a promise and a reminder that whether we are near or miles apart, our love for them grows and strengthens with every day."[1]

As I listened to the song, I thought that's how it should be with our young adult children—we should be there to hold them when they need it, but never hold them back. We should be the ones by their side, cheering them on, but letting them decide their steps. As the song says, "I could be the one to let you choose." What a gift to be the one to empower our young adult children's choices! And it goes on to describe a beautiful and wild life—just like a river—but asks, "Who am I to take control of that?"

The song is full of assurances that we don't have to do life alone and swirls around the theme that we just want to flow along with the person we love so dearly. And that is my encouragement and charge to you dear momma: Be the banks of your young adult children's lives. Hold them close, but don't hold them back. Be a voice they can follow; be a place they can rest. But let them be their own river—not needing a push or pull, just needing banks to hold them. You can do this—you *get* to do this—so make it your mission to do it *well*. I believe in you!

*It is not what you do for your children, but what you have taught them
to do for themselves that will make them successful human beings.*
Ann Landers

NOTES

1. PERSPECTIVE MATTERS

1. "What does it mean when Jesus says, 'My yoke is easy and my burden is light?'," Got Questions, May 13, 2024, https://www.gotquestions.org/yoke-easy-burden-light.html.
2. Galatians 5:1
3. Psalm 105:4

2. GRIEF IS AN EXPRESSION OF LOVE

1. Ruth Hardy, "Advise for parents: how to say goodbye when your child leaves home," The Guardian, September 18, 2013, https:// https://www.theguardian.com/education/2013/sep/18/parents-coping-when-children-leave-home.
2. Catherine Naja, "The Grief in Growing Up," HuffPost, December 6, 2017, https://www.huffpost.com/entry/the-grief-in-growing-up_b_7206488.
3. Whitney Fleming, author of *You're Not a Failure: My Teen Doesn't Like Me Either*, https://www.facebook.com/whitneyflemingwrites.
4. "10 Quotes from Billy Graham on grief," The Billy Graham Library, September 6, 2019, https://www.billygrahamlibrary.org/blog-10-quotes-from-billy-graham-on-grief/.
5. 2 Corinthians 1:3-4
6. Jessica Halloway, "Grief is the Profound Testament to the Depth of Our Love," Psychreg, August 18, 2023, https://www.psychreg.org/grief-profound-testament-depth-love/#The-silver-lining.

3. A JOURNEY OF STAGES

1. The six stages are: Image-Making Stage, Nurturing Stage, Authority Stage, Interpretive Stage, Interdependent Stage, Departure Stage.
2. Bob Hostetler, "The Four Phases of Parenthood," Focus on the Family, June 2007, https://www.focusonthefamily.com/parenting/the-four-phases-of-parenthood/.
3. Ibid
4. Sheri R, "17 inspiring quotes to live by," care., July 9, 2024, https://www.care.com/c/inspirational-parenting-quotes/.
5. "How to let go of your adult children when you're struggling to detach," A Modern Life, September 8, 2022, https://amodernmidlife.com/how-to-let-go-of-your-adult-children-when-youre-struggling-to-detach/.

6. Annie Reneau, "Kids Growing Up is the Best and Worst Thing," Scary Mommy, May 19, 2017, https:// www.scarymommy.com/kids-growing-up-heartache-joy.

7. Tim Dowling, "They take over your life and then, one day, they walk off with it: life before and after children," The Guardian, January 23, 2016, www.theguardian.com/lifeandstyle/2016/jan/23/life-before-and-after-children-tim-dowling.

8. Denise Gorant, host. "A New Perspective: You and Your Adult Child with Dr. Laurence Steinberg." *Bite Your Tongue,* 6 October 2023, https:// www.biteyourtonguepodcast.com/season-3-episode-59-a-new-perspective-you-and-your-adult-child-with-dr-laurence-steinberg/.

4. TRUST ISN'T BLIND FAITH

1. Joan Ryan, *The Water Giver: The Story of a Mother, a Son, and Their Second Chance* (New York, NY: Simon & Schuster, 2010).

2. Ibid

3. C. Dwight Bain, "Parenting Launch Sequence—Letting Go of Children so they can Launch as successful Adults," LinkedIn, January 19, 20222, https://www.linkedin.com/pulse/parenting-launch-sequence-letting-go-children-so-can-dwight/.

4. Anna Meade Harris, "Parenting is a Progressive Letting Go," Rooted Ministry, April 7, 2021, https://www. rootedministry.com/parenting-progressive-letting-go/.

5. ADULTHOOD IS THE SCARIEST HOOD

1. Julie Lythcott-Haimes, "The Over-Parenting Trap: How to Avoid 'Checklisted' Childhoods and Raise Adults," TIME, June 9, 2015, https:// www.time.com/3910020/the-over-parenting-trap-how-to-avoid-checklisted-childhoods-and-raise-adults/.

2. This term refers to the season of life for parents who have launched their children into adulthood—also known as the empty nest.

3. Jim Burns, *Doing Life with Your Adult Children,* (Grand Rapids, MI: Zondervan, 2019), 97.

4. Dr. Jane Adams, *When Our Grown Kids Disappoint Us,* (Free Press, New York, NY: 2003), 13.

5. Ibid, 12.

6. Jim Burns, *Doing Life With Your Adult Children,* (Grand Rapids, MI: Zondervan, 2019), 99-100.

7. Deanna Brann, "Is Your Son Pulling Away? Get The Real Reason He May Be Doing So," HuffPost, December 6, 2017, https://www.huffpost.com/entry/is-your-son-pulling-away_b_5247495.

8. Shelby Cormier, "The Beauty of the Constantly Evolving Mother-Daughter Relationship," May 11, 2021, darling Society, https://blog.darlingsociety.com/the-beauty-of-the-constantly-evolving-mother-daughter-relationship.

9. Jamie Kenney, "13 Moms on What It's Like to Watch Your Baby Grow," Romper, January 26, 2017, https://www.romper.com/p/13-moms-describe-what-its-like-to-watch-your-baby-grow-up-33083.

10. Emily Freeman, "What It Feels Like When Your Kids Are Growing Up," Emily P Freeman, https://www.emilypfreeman.com.

11. Annie Reneau, "Kids Growing Up Is The Best And Worst Thing," Scarry Mommy, May 19, 2017, https://www.scarymommy.com/kids-growing-up-heartache-joy.

12. Mia Freedman, "Your son growing up will feel like the slowest breakup you've ever known," Mamamia, November 23, 2019, https://www.mamamia.com.au/mia-freedman-family/.

6. LESS IS SUCCESS

1. Jackson Msiop, "Adult Children: When to Help and When to Let Them Learn," We Have Kids, July 21, 2023, https://wehavekids.com/family-relationships/Adult-Children-When-to-Help-When-to-Let-Them-Learn.

2. Cory Stieg, "Kids with 'helicopter parents' more likely to burn out, have a harder time transitioning to 'real world'," November 22, 2019, https://www.cnbc.com/2019/11/22/study-kids-who-have-helicopter-parents-experience-burnout-in-school.html.

3. "Helicopter Parent," Wikipedia, January 2023, https://www. en.wikipedia.org/wiki/Helicopter_parent.

4. Millenials are defined as people born beteen 1981 to 1996.

5. "Helicopter Parent Who Delayed Their Kids Development, Now May Be Paying Cruel Price," Our Town, August 3, 2023, https://www.ourtownny.com/news/helicopter-parents-who-delayed-their-kids-development-now-may-be-paying-cruel-price-DD2656984.

6. David Von Drehle, *The Book of Charlie: Wisdom From the Remarkable American Life of a 109-Year-Old Man,* (New York, NY, Simon and Schuster, May 23, 2023), 95.

7. Dr. Jane Adams, *When Our Grown Kids Disappoint Us,* (Free Press, New York, NY: 2003), 48.

8. "Current Economic Climate Drives More Than Half of Gen Z To Live With Their Parents," News Wire, November 15, 2022, https://www.prnewswire.com/news-releases/current-economic-climate-drives-more-than-half-of-gen-z-to-live-with-their-parents-301678724.html.

9. Jackson Msiop, "Adult Children: When to Help and When to Let Them Learn," We Have Kids, July 21, 2023, https://wehavekids.com/family-relationships/Adult-Children-When-to-Help-When-to-Let-Them-Learn.

10. "Nearly 4 in 10 Employers Avoid Hiring Recent College Grads in Favor of Older Workers," Intelligent, December 12, 2023, https://www.intelligent.com/nearly-4-in-10-employers-avoid-hiring-recent-college-grads-in-favor-of-older-workers/.

11. April Brewer, "How to Stop Enabling Grown Children and Why It's Important," Better Help, July 4, 2024, https://www.betterhelp.com/advice/family/how-to-stop-enabling-grown-children-and-why-its-important/.

12. Dylan Banks, "10 Helpful Ways to Connect With Your Struggling Adult Child," Marriage, March 1, 2024, https://www.marriage.com/advice/parenting/struggling-adult-child/.

13. Dr. Jane Adams, *When Our Grown Kids Disappoint Us*, (New York, NY: Free Press, 2003), 29.

7. HOW HEALTHY ARE WE?

1. Madhuleena Roy Chowdhury, "The Neuroscience of Gratitude and Effects on the Brain," Positive Psychology, April 9, 2019, https://positivepsychology.com/neuroscience-of-gratitude/.

2. Jeff Manion, *The Land Between: Finding God in Difficult Transitions* (Zondervan, Grand Rapids, MI, 2012).

3. Isaiah 43:19

4. Scott Hubbard, "God Awakens Us In The Desert," Desiring God, March 6, 2019, https://www.desiringgod.org/articles/god-awakens-us-in-the-wilderness.

5. Matthew 7:7-8

6. Dr. Wayne Dyer, https://www.drwaynedyer.com.

8. MADE FOR A PURPOSE

1. Alice Hoekstra, "5 Questions To Help You Find Your Purpose," Thrive Global, July 13, 2018, https://www. community.thriveglobal.com/what-is-a-purpose/.

2. LJ Herman, "'I have 7 children. They do not give me purpose and meaning. My world does not revolve around them.': Mom finds meaning beyond her children, 'I will not burden them with being my universe,'" Love Matters, February 9, 2022, https://www.lovewhatmatters.com/i-have-7-children-they-do-not-give-me-purpose-and-meaning-my-world-does-not-revolve-around-them-mom-finds-meaning-beyond-her-children-i-will-not-burden-them-with-being/.

3. Tracy Otsuka, "I Thought Parenting Was My Life's Purpose: I Was Wrong," HuffPost, April 29, 2016, https://www.huffpost.com/entry/i-thought-parenting-was-m_b_9808792.

4. Christine Hammond, "The Primary Purpose of Parenting," PsychCentral, August 3, 2016, https://psychcentral.com/pro/exhausted-woman/2016/08/the-primary-purpose-of-parenting#1.

5. Micah 6:8

6. Genesis 1:28

7. Ecclesiastes 12:13

8. Alice Hoekstra, "5 Questions To Help You Find Your Purpose," Thrive Global, July 13, 2018, https://www. community.thriveglobal.com/what-is-a-purpose/.

9. Ibid

10. Ibid

11. Matthew 7:7-8, NLT

9. LOVING A PRODIGAL

1. Diane Chamberlain, *The Secret Life of CeeCee Wilkes*, (New York, NY: Mira Books, 2006) 257.
2. James 1:20
3. Liz Snell, "A Liturgy When Someone You Love Believes Differently Than You," *Every Moment Holy, Volume 3*, (Nashville, TN: Rabbit Room Press, 2023) 226-229.
4. Dr. Jane Adams, *When Our Grown Kids Disappoint Us*, (New York, NY: Free Press, 2003), 149-150.
5. William P. Young, *The Shack*, (New York City: NY Hachette Book Group, 2007).

AFTERWORD

1. Song Facts, 2020, https://www.songfacts.com/facts/needtobreathe/banks.

ACKNOWLEDGMENTS

There are so many people to thank—the list is longer than space allows—but I would be remiss to not say thank you here to these incredible people.

To Tim, for choosing to do life with me and joining me on this adventure we call parenthood. You are the first to offer grace, encouragement, and prayer to each one of us. You're a superb dad, and I am blessed to be your wife. I still do!

To Emma and Nate, the answers to my prayers when I wanted to be a mom. What a gift you are to me and this world! Thank you for making motherhood my favorite part of life. My heart swells with joy at the mention of your names. Always remember who you are; remember whose you are.

To Marcus, an old friend who became a new friend. Thank you for giving me the opportunity to live in my purpose and for spurring me on when I was learning the steps. Your gift of encouragement is unparalleled.

To Jenn, Jill, and Tracy, for taking this journey with me. As my sounding board and first readers, your feedback has been invaluable, and your friendship is priceless.

ABOUT THE AUTHOR

Wife and mother of two, Cristina Wright is a former homeschool mom turned book editor and writer who loves waterskiing, riding motorcycles, and running. She is a lover of Jesus, tacos, and books. As a Texas native who loves her life in Colorado, Cristina likes to say she is Texas deep and Colorado tall. *Launch Them Well* is her first book.

www.ingramcontent.com/pod-product-compliance
Lightning Source LLC
Chambersburg PA
CBHW071445130726
47997CB00006B/2240